EVERY STEP I[I]

THE COLD-PACK METHOD

BY

GRACE VIALL GRAY, PH.B., ED.B

Formerly Associate Professor of Home Economics, Iowa State College

Originally published in 1920.

PREFACE

It was six years ago that I first heard of the One Period, Cold-Pack Method of canning. A little circular was put in my hand one day at a federated club meeting announcing the fact that in a few weeks there would be a cold-pack demonstration about fifty miles away. Immediately I announced that I was going to the demonstrations. So leaving my small daughter with my mother, I went to the Normal School at DeKalb, Illinois, and heard and saw for the first time cold-pack canning.

It is sufficient to say that those three days were so crowded full of interest and new messages on the gospel of canning that I felt amply repaid for going fifty miles. As a result of that trip, the first story ever published on cold-pack canning appeared in *The Country Gentleman* and I had the pleasure of writing it. So enthused was I over this new, efficient and easy way to can not only fruits but hard vegetables, such as peas, corn and beans, that I wanted to carry the good news into the kitchen of other busy housewives and mothers.

My mother had insisted that I take with me my younger sister, just from college, but with no domestic science tendencies. So, much against her wishes, preferring rather to do some settlement work, my sister went with me. The canning was so interesting that for the first time in her life, my sister became enthusiastic over one phase of cooking. My mother was so pleased at this zeal that when she received my sister's letter written from DeKalb, saying, "Mother, I am enthused about this canning and want to can everything in sight this summer," she hastily washed all available glass jars and tops and had everything in readiness for young daughter's return. And we canned. We were not content to can alone but invited all the neighbors in and taught them how to can. Our community canned more things and more unusual things, including the hard vegetables, that year than they had ever attempted before.

Do not think for one minute it was all easy sailing, for there were doubting Thomases, but it only took time and *results* to convert even the most skeptical ones. And here I must make a confession. It was much easier for my sister, unversed in any phase of canning, to master this new method than it was for me with my four years' training course and my five years of teaching canning behind me. And this is the reason. She had nothing to "unlearn," she knew no other method whereas I had to "unlearn" all my previous methods.

The one period, cold-pack method is so entirely different from the old hot pack or open kettle method that to be successful you must forget all you ever knew and be willing to be taught anew. And right here is where many women "fall down"— they are not willing to admit that they know nothing about it and so do not get accurate information about it. They are so afraid of appearing ignorant. This false feeling is the greatest obstacle in woman's way.

I still go into small towns on my lecture trips and women will say, "Oh, that cold-pack canning isn't new to me. I have used it for thirty years." And when I show my surprise, they further enlighten me with, "and my mother used it before me, too." With a little tactful questioning I usually get these answers: "Of course, I do not hot dip and cold dip. I never heard of that before. I pack the products into the cold jars and for all vegetables I use a preserving powder because there is no way on earth to keep corn and peas and such things unless you put something into them to keep them. Fruit will keep all right. Then I cook them in my wash boiler until they are done." And when I ask, "How do you know when they are done," I invariably get the answer, "Oh, I take out a jar once in a while and try it." It seems like such a hopeless task to change all these old-fashioned, out-of-date methods of cooking but with a great amount of patience and much actual canning it can usually be done. Not always, of course, for there are some women who seem to delight in sticking to the old rather than try the new.

The present book is therefore designed for all interested in greater efficiency in the home, including not only students of home economics but all persons who have charge of homes and are interested in learning new, efficient, time and labor saving methods.

In the preparation of this book I have received much help from Mr. O.H. Benson, Agriculturist in charge of the government Boys' and Girls' Club Work, and my first instructor in Cold-Pack Canning. I also wish to acknowledge my appreciation to those who have helped to make this book possible by contributing information, advice and encouragement.

GRACE VIALL GRAY.
October, 1919.

CONTENTS

CHAPTER I

GETTING READY TO CAN

Before the World War, housewives had lost the good habit of canning, preserving and pickling. It was easier to buy California fruits by the case and canned vegetables by the dozen or half dozen cans, according to the size of the family. There is no doubt it was cheaper and decidedly easier to purchase canned fruits, vegetables, greens, soups and meats than to take time and strength in the very hottest season of the year to do our own canning.

But what was true then is not true now. The war taught us thrift. The crime of wasting even a few tomatoes or berries has sunk into our minds to stay forever; scientific canning methods have been adopted by the modern woman. Women who had never canned in days before the war had to can during war days. Food was so scarce and so high in price that to buy fancy or even plain canned products was a severe strain on the average housewife's purse. The American woman, as was to be expected, came quickly and eagerly to the front with the solution and the slogan: "More gardens and more canning and preserving at home."

A great garden and canning movement swept the whole country. As I have just said, women who had never canned before became vitally interested in putting up not merely a few jars of this and that, but jars upon jars of canned fruits, vegetables and greens; and so great was their delight in the finished products that again and again

I heard them say: "Never again shall we depend upon the grocery to supply us with canned goods."

If these women had been obliged to use the same methods that their grandmothers used before them, they would have canned just the same, because it was their patriotic duty to do so; but they would have canned without the enthusiasm and zeal that was so apparent during the summers of 1917 and 1918. This enthusiasm was a result of new canning methods, methods unknown to our grandmothers. The women of to-day were forced into a new field and learned how satisfying and well worth while the results were. It is safe to guarantee that every home-canning recruit will become a home-canning veteran.

The fascination of doing one's own canning after one has learned how simple and economical it is will be lasting. No one need fear that home canning is going to suffer because the war ended the immediate necessity for it. Home canning has come into its own because of the war, and it has come to stay because of its many merits.

There are four methods of canning that are employed by women all over the United States. They are the "open-kettle," the "intermittent," the "cold-water" and the "cold-pack" methods.

DRAWBACKS OF THE OLD METHODS

The "open-kettle," or "hot-pack," method is the oldest. It was largely used in the pre-war days. The food is completely cooked in the preserving kettle, and is then packed into hot, sterilized jars, after which the jars are sealed. As the packing into the jar is done after the sterilization has been completed, there is always a possibility of bacteria and spores entering the jar with the cooked food and the air. Fruits can be handled successfully in this way, but this method cannot be used for vegetables, greens and meats. It is a very laborious, hot and hard way to can. Modern housewives are discarding it more and more every year and are beginning to place their trust in the newer and far more scientific methods of canning.

The "intermittent," or fractional sterilization, method is still beloved by some people who cling to the sure and hate to venture into the new. Vegetables can be handled by this method as can all fruits and meats. It is used rather extensively in the South, where they say the conditions do not favor "cold-pack." The great objection to this method of canning is that it requires three periods of sterilization on three different days and three liftings of jars in and out of the sterilizer.

What is sometimes called the "cold-water" method of canning should not be confused with the "cold-pack" method. The "cold-water" is often used in connection with the canning of rhubarb, green gooseberries and a comparatively few other sour berry fruits. If the "cold-water" method is used we would suggest that the product be thoroughly washed, placed in a strainer, scalding water poured over it, and the product then packed at once, in practically a fresh state, in the jars, and clean, cold water applied until the jars are filled. If these steps are taken carefully and quickly the method in most cases will be successful with such acid products as I mentioned. As the products will have to be cooked before they can be used many housewives do not consider it any saving of time or labor to follow this method.

THE COLD-PACK METHOD

The method of to-day that came into its own during the war is known as the "cold-pack" method of canning. It fought a long fight to prove that it was a very efficient, economical and satisfactory process for busy housewives to can everything that grows.

This is the method that I shall mostly refer to in this book, and if I should omit the phrase "cold-pack" you will know that I am referring to it. "Cold-pack" simply means that the products are packed cold in their fresh and natural state in the glass jars or containers. To the fruits hot sirup is applied; to the vegetables hot water and a little salt are added. The sterilization is done in the glass jars or tin containers after they are partly or entirely sealed, making it practically impossible for bacteria or spores to enter after the product has once been carefully sterilized or cooked. In following this method vegetables should first be blanched in boiling water or live steam, then quickly plunged into cold water and the skins removed. The products are then packed in containers and sterilized according to the instructions and recipes given later.

When we use the term sterilizing we simply mean cooking the product for a certain period of time after the jar has been filled with food. It is sometimes called processing. Sterilizing, processing, boiling and cooking are all interchangeable terms and mean one and the same thing.

By this "cold-pack," or cold-fill, method of canning, all food products, including fruits, vegetables and meats, can be successfully sterilized in a single period with but one handling of the product in and out of the canner.

All the flavor is retained, the product is not cooked to a mushy pulp, and the labor and time needed for the canning are less than in any other method. The housewife's canning enemy, mold, is eliminated and all bacteria and bacterial spores which cause vegetables and meat to spoil are destroyed.

EXPENSIVE OUTFITS NOT ESSENTIAL

For this "cold-pack" method you can use whatever equipment you have in the kitchen. Complicated equipment is not essential. Many of us have purchased commercial outfits, for we know we can turn out more at the end of a day and have found it well worth while to invest a few dollars in equipment that enabled us to be more efficient. But if you are a beginner and do not care to put any money in an unknown venture use the available things at hand, just to prove to yourself and others that it can be done.

Every type of glass jar manufactured can be used except those which are sealed with wax. So dig into your storerooms, attics and basements and bring forth all your old jars. If a top is in good condition and will make a perfect seal when adjusted with a good rubber you can use that jar.

If the tops cannot be restored to good

condition it is poor economy to use them. Imperfectly sealed jars are probably responsible for more spoiled canned goods than any other cause. Good tops and good rubbers are requisites for good canning.

For your canner, or sterilizer, you may use a wash boiler or a galvanized bucket, such as is used for a garbage pail—a new one, of course. Either is excellent where the family is small and the canning is accordingly light. Some use the reservoir of the cookstove while others employ a large vat. If you should have to buy the wash boiler or pail see that it has a tight-fitting cover and be sure the pail does not leak. Then all you have to do is to secure what we call a false bottom, something that will keep the jars of fruit from touching the direct bottom of the boiler or pail. This false bottom, remember, is absolutely necessary, for without it the jars will break during the boiling.

For this false bottom use a wire netting of half-inch mesh and cut it to fit the bottom of the sterilizer, whether boiler, pail or bucket. If you haven't any netting and do not care to purchase it a wooden bottom can be made to fit the sterilizer, or if that is not available put thin pieces of wood in the bottom—anything to keep the jars from coming in direct contact with the bottom of the sterilizer.

If you have only a small quantity of berries or fruit to can use a deep saucepan with a tight-fitting cover and a few slats of wood. This rack is absolutely necessary to keep the contents of the jars from becoming overheated. Even if they should not break there is a tendency for part of the contents to escape under the cover and be lost. Do not use hay, old clothes, newspapers or excelsior for a false bottom; they are unsatisfactory because they do not allow proper circulation of water.

Individual jar holders are very convenient and are preferred by many women to the racks. Inexpensive racks with handles are on the market and are worth what they cost in saved nerves and unburned fingers. Some hold eight jars, others hold twelve. So it just lies with you, individual housekeeper, whether you want a rack that will hold all your jars or a set of individual holders that handles them separately.

To return to the subject of the canner, let me add that no matter what kind you use, it must be at least three inches deeper than the tallest jar. This will give room for the rack and an extra inch or two so that the water will not boil over.

Besides the canners, the jars, the rubber rings and the rack you will need one kettle for boiling water, into which the product may be put for scalding or blanching; another kettle for water—if you haven't running water—for the "cold dip."

If you use a homemade rack without handles you should have a jar lifter of some kind for placing in and removing jars from the canner. If individual holders are used this is not necessary, as they contain an upright bail. Some women use a wire potato masher for lifting the jars out of the canners. Other kitchen equipment, such as scales, knives, spoons, wire basket or a piece of cheesecloth or muslin for blanching or scalding the product, and the kitchen clock play their part in canning.

No canning powder or any preservative is needed. If the product is cooked in closed jars in the hot-water bath as directed the food will be sterilized so that it will keep indefinitely. If it is desired to add salt, sugar, sirup, vinegar or other flavor this may be done when the product is packed in the jar.

A great many people have been led to believe through advertising matter that it is both safe and practical to use canning compounds for the preserving of vegetables which have proved hard to keep under the commonly known methods of canning. The first argument against the use of a canning compound is that it is unnecessary. It is possible to sterilize any fruit or vegetable which grows on tree, vine, shrub or in the ground by this cold-pack, single-period method of canning, without the use of a compound. The second argument against it is that many of the canning compounds are positively harmful to health. Some of them contain as high as ninety-five per cent of boric acid. Directors of county and state fairs should exclude from entry all fruits and vegetables that have been preserved in any canning compound. Perfect fruit can be produced without any chemical preservative. The third argument is that they are expensive.

There are many modifications of the original wash boiler and garbage pail cookers. These are all known as the hot-water-bath outfits. In these outfits the products are all cooked in boiling water.

There are condensed-steam cookers under various names, where the product is cooked in condensed steam. These steamers are generally used for everyday cookery.

The water-seal outfit, the steam-pressure outfit and the aluminum pressure cooker follow in order of efficiency as regards the time required to sterilize food.

Following the hot-water canner in simplicity

of construction and manipulation is the water-seal
cooker. The temperature of the hot-water-seal outfit
is a little higher than the homemade or hot-water-
bath outfit; so time is saved in the sterilizing.

The steam-pressure and the pressure cookers
are more complicated but more efficient. Some
prefer the aluminum pressure cooker because it can
be used for everyday cooking in the home.

Pressure cookers are expensive, but they are
worth their price, as they are used daily and not just
during the canning season.

Here are examples of how they rank as to
time required: In a hot-water-bath outfit soft fruits
must be sterilized sixteen minutes; in a steamer,
sixteen minutes; in a water-seal outfit, twelve
minutes; in a steam-pressure-outfit under five
pounds of steam, ten minutes; in an aluminum
pressure cooker outfit with ten pounds of steam,
five minutes.

It takes longest to can with a homemade or
hot-water-bath outfit; the shortest and quickest
method is with the pressure cooker that has a
pressure of ten pounds or more. Each housewife has
different financial problems, different hours of
working and different ways of working. Where
quick work is desired and expense is no item the
pressure cooker is advisable; where money is scarce
and time is no object the homemade outfit answers.
Each one must decide which outfit is best for her
own particular case. It matters not which outfit you
have—they have all been thoroughly tested and
approved by experts. Each one does the work.

This equipment for canning should be in all
kitchens: four-quart kettle for blanching; steamer
for steaming greens; colander; quart measure;

funnel; good rubber rings; sharp paring knives; jar opener; wire basket and a piece of cheesecloth one yard square for blanching; pineapple scissors; one large preserving spoon; one tablespoon; one teaspoon; one set of measuring spoons; measuring cup; jar lifter; either a rack for several jars or individual jar holders; and a clock.

The manufacturers, realizing that boys and girls must be kept busy during the vacation months, have made some wonderful devices for outdoor canning. Would it not be a good plan to buy one for the young people of your family and give them something definite and worth while to do in summer? You know little brains and hands must be kept busy—if not usefully employed they are often inclined to mischief. This type of cooker furnishes its own heat; so it can be used in the back yard, in the orchard or under the trees in the front yard.

Remember that the higher the altitude the lower the degree of heat required to boil water. Time-tables given in instructions for canning are usually based upon the requirements of an altitude of 500 feet above sea level. Generally speaking, for every 4000-foot increase in altitude it will be well to add twenty per cent to the time required as given in recipes or time schedules for the canning of all kinds of fruits, vegetables, greens and meats.

CHAPTER II

SOFT FRUITS AND BERRIES

Having decided on your canning outfit, whether you are going to can in boiling water, in a condensed steam cooker, or in steam under pressure; having gathered together the necessary tools, such as spoons, knives and a funnel; having raided the storeroom and collected some jars, you are now ready for the actual work of canning.

It is rather unfortunate that strawberries should be one of the very hardest products to can with good results. The canning itself is simple—all berries are quickly and easily canned—but strawberries always shrink, are apt to turn a little brown, and, what distresses us most of all, they float to the top of the jar.

The berry's tendency to shrink is responsible for loss of color as well as its floating qualities. However, if you will be exceedingly careful to remove the berries from the canner the minute the clock says the sterilizing period is over, you will have a fairly good product. Two minutes too long will produce a very dark, shrunken berry. So be careful of the cooking time. Another thing that makes a good-looking jar is to pack a quart of berries—all kinds of berries, not merely strawberries—into a pint jar. If you will get that many in you will have a much better-looking jar, with very little liquid at the bottom. It does not hurt the berries at all to gently press down on them with a silver spoon while you are packing them into the jar.

We know we are going to get a quart of berries into every pint jar, so we know just how many quarts of berries we will need to fill the necessary jars for the next winter's use.

The first thing to do is to test each jar to see that there are no cracks, no rough edges to cut the rubber, and to see whether the cover and clamp fit tightly, if a clamp type of jar is used. The bail that clamps down the glass tops should go down with a good spring. If it does not, remove the bail and bend it into shape by taking it in both hands and pressing down in the middle with both thumbs. Do not bend it too hard, for if it goes down with too much of a snap it will break the jar. This testing of the bails should be done every year. The bails on new jars are sometimes too tight, in which case remove the bail and spread it out. After the bail has been readjusted, test it again. The chances are it will be just right. Of course all this testing takes time, but it pays.

If you are using some old Mason jars put a rubber on each jar, fill the jar with hot water, and then put the cover on tight and invert. This is a sure test for leakage. Never use a Mason cap twice unless the cover and collar are separate so that both can be completely sterilized. Fortunately the old-fashioned Mason jar metal cover to which a porcelain cap is fastened is going out of style.

If you still have some of these old covers it will be economy to throw them away. You will be money ahead in the end. After these tops have been used once it is impossible to make a fastening between the porcelain and the metal so tight that it is not possible for the liquid to seep through and cause the contents to spoil. This accounts for many failures when old tops are used. For this reason never use the old-fashioned, zinc-topped covers.

The new and safe Mason jar covers consist of two parts, the metal collar and the porcelain cap. They are for sale at all grocery or hardware stores.

If you are using the vacuum-seal jars which have a composition attached to the lacquered tops, carefully examine this rubber composition to see that it is perfect. This composition should go entirely round the top and should not be cut or broken in any place. If it is the top must be discarded for a perfect one.

Of course with this type of jar no rubber rings are necessary, as the rubber composition on the lacquered top does the sealing.

It is a wise plan to go round the tops and over the inside of all new glass jars with a heavy and dull knife to scrape off any slivers of glass or bursted blisters that may be still clinging to the jars. Those on the tops cut through the rubber and cause leakage. Those in the jars may get into the product. I often find these splinters, particularly on new straight-sided jars.

It matters not what type of jar you use. Use what you have at hand, but if you are buying new jars consider the following things before making your selections: No metal, unless it is enameled or lacquered, should come in contact with the food. The jars should be of smooth, well-finished glass. The color of the jar does not affect the keeping qualities of the food. The top or part of the top that comes in contact with the contents should be all in one piece, so as not to offer a place for the accumulation of organisms and dirt. The jars which have nearly straight sides and a wide mouth or opening are easier to wash and facilitate better, quicker and easier packing of the product.

Wash the jars in soap and water. Rinse in boiling water. Some people temper new jars so they will stand the shock of hot water or hot sirup without breaking. If you wish to take this extra precaution put the jars in a dishpan or kettle of cold water after they have been washed in soapy water; bring the water slowly to a boil and let it boil fifteen minutes. After the jars are ready test the rubber rings. This may seem a useless precaution, but it is a necessary one, for there is no one detail in the business of canning that is more important. Even in the best boxes of rubbers there is occasionally a black sheep, and one black sheep may cause the loss of a jar.

Test each rubber before you use it by pressing it firmly between the thumbs and forefingers, stretching it very slightly. If it seems soft and spongy discard it. All rubbers fit for canning should be firm, elastic, and should endure a stretching pull without breaking. A good rubber ring will return promptly to place without changing the inside diameter.

A great many women are laboring under the wrong impression that color affects the quality of a ring. Some women insist on red, and others on white. Color is given to rings by adding coloring matter during the manufacturing process. The color of the ring is no index to its usefulness in home canning.

Use only fresh, sound strawberries or other berries. There is a little knack about preparing the strawberries that few housewives know. Hull the berries by *twisting the berries off the hull*, instead of pulling the hull from the berry as most women do. You will have a better-looking berry if you will be careful about this. Place the berries in a strainer and pour cold water over them to cleanse them.

HOW TO ADJUST THE COVERS

Never allow the berries or any fruit to stand in water, as the flavor and color are destroyed by water-soaking. Pack in glass jars, pressing the berries down tightly, but without crushing them. Put the rubber on the jar if you are using a jar requiring a rubber. Pour hot sirup over the berries. Put the top of the jar in place, but only partially tighten it.

If using the screw-top jars, such as the Mason, screw down with the thumb and little finger, not using force but stopping when the cover catches.

If using vacuum-seal jars put the cover on and the spring in place. The spring will give enough to allow the steam to escape.

In using glass-top jars with the patent wire snap, put the cover in place, the wire over the top and leave the clamp up.

The cover on a glass jar must not be tight while the product is cooking, because the air will expand when heated, and if the cover is not loose enough to allow the steam to escape the pressure may blow the rubber out or break the jar.

The product is now ready for the canner.

STERILIZING

If you are using the homemade outfit, such as wash-boiler or garbage pail, all berries and soft fruits are sterilized sixteen minutes; in all commercial hot-water-bath outfits and in condensed steam, sixteen minutes; in the water-seal, twelve minutes; in the steam pressure under five pounds of steam, ten minutes; and in the pressure cooker under ten pounds of steam, five minutes. Do not allow the pressure to run above ten pounds for soft fruits; fifteen pounds makes them mushy.

If you use any type of hot-water-bath outfit be sure the water is boiling when the fruit is lowered into the canner, and *keep it boiling* vigorously for the entire sixteen minutes. At the end of the sterilizing time, *immediately* remove the jars from the canner.

In taking canned goods from boiling water care is needed to see that they are protected from drafts. If necessary close the windows and doors while lifting the jars out, as a sudden draft might break them.

Examine rubbers to see that they are in place. Sometimes if a cover is screwed down too tight the pressure of the steam from the inside causes the rubber to bulge out. Simply loosen the cover a thread or two, push the rubber back into place and then tighten.

In case the rubber does not seem to fit well or seems to be a poor rubber it should be replaced by a new one, and the jar returned to the cooker for five minutes.

The jars should be sealed tight—covers screwed down, clamps put in place—immediately after they are removed from the cooker.

Invert the jar to test the joint, then let it cool. If the seal is not perfect correct the fault and return the jar to the cooker for five minutes if hot, ten minutes if the jar is cold.

Do not invert vacuum-seal jars. These should be allowed to cool, and then be tested by removing the spring or clamp and lifting the jars by the cover only. Lift the jar only half an inch, holding it over the table, so that in case the lid does not hold the jar and contents will not be damaged. Or, better still, tap round the edge of the cover with a rule. An imperfect seal will give a hollow sound.

As light injures delicately colored fruits and vegetables, it is wise to store them in dark places, such as cupboards, or basement or attic shelves protected from the light. Black cambric tacked to the top shelf and suspended over the other shelves is a sufficient protection from light. A discarded window shade can be rolled down over the shelves and easily pulled up when you desire to take a jar from the shelves.

Canned goods are best kept at a temperature below seventy degrees Fahrenheit, where that is at all possible.

STEPS IN CANNING SOFT FRUITS AND BERRIES

It might be well to enumerate the steps in berry and soft-fruit canning, or do what we called in our schooldays "review it":

1. Get the canner and all its accessories ready.

2. Test and wash jars and tops and put in water to sterilize.

3. Test rubber rings.

4. Make sirup and put in double boiler to keep hot

5. Prepare the product—hull, seed, stem.

6. Place berries or fruit in strainer or colander.

7. Rinse by pouring cold water over product.

8. Pack from strainer into hot jar.

9. Use big spoon to get a firm pack.

10. Dip rubber in hot water to cleanse it and put it in place on the jar.

11. Pour the hot sirup over the fruit at once.

12. Put top of jar on, but not tight.

13. Ready for canner.

14. Sterilize for the necessary length of time, according to the outfit you are using:
MINUTES Hot-water-bath outfit 16 Condensed-steam outfit 16 Water-seal outfit 12 Steam pressure, 5 pounds, outfit 10 Pressure cooker, 10 pounds, outfit 5   15. Remove from canner.

16. Tighten cover, except vacuum-seal jar, which seals automatically.

17. Test joint.

18. Three or four days later, if perfectly air-tight, label and store in a dark place.

These steps are followed for strawberries, blackberries, blueberries, dewberries, huckleberries, gooseberries, raspberries, and for all soft fruits, such as cherries, currants, grapes and figs.

The other soft fruits, such as peaches and apricots, which have a skin, are scalded or "hot dipped" for one to two minutes in boiling water or steam and are then plunged into cold water. These two steps of hot-dipping and cold dipping make the removal of skins a very simple operation. After the skins are removed the fruit is put into the hot jars and the process continued from Step 8, as with strawberries.

SIRUPS

Of course you are wondering about the sirups for the different fruits. There is no set rule for making sirup. It is not necessary to use sirup in canning fruits. The amount of sugar used in the sirup will depend upon the individual taste. In a first-class product there should be enough sirup to improve its flavor, but not enough to make it take the place in the diet of a sweet preserve rather than a fresh fruit.

The sirups are made either with varying proportions of sugar and water or with the same proportions boiled different lengths of time. What is known as the California sirup is made with three parts of sugar to two parts of water, boiled gently to different concentrations.

Thin Sirup. For a thin sirup take three cups of sugar and two cups of water. Mix sugar and heat until the sugar is dissolved. This is used for all sweet fruits not too delicate in texture and color, as apples, cherries, pears, or for fruits in which more sugar will be added in preparation for the table.

Medium Thin Sirup. The sugar and water should be boiled about four minutes, or until it begins to be sirupy. This is used for raspberries, peaches, blackberries, currants, etc.

Medium Thick Sirup. Boil the sugar and

water until it will pile up over the edge of the spoon when it is tipped. This is used for sour or acid fruits, as plums, gooseberries, apricots, sour apples, and some of the delicately colored fruits, as strawberries.

Thick Sirup. The sugar and water are boiled until it will form a ball in the spoon and cannot be poured from the spoon. This is used for preserves.

It is possible to get more, sometimes almost twice as much, sirup into a quart jar containing large fruits, as apples and pears, than into a quart jar containing small fruits, as currants or blackberries.

There is a little knack worth knowing about combining the sugar and water for the sirup. If the sugar is sifted into the boiling water just as fine-grained cereals are sifted into water, there will be no scum formed. This is a saving of sugar.

If you wish to can strawberries for the market or to win a prize at the county or state fairs, can them as follows:

Canned by this recipe, strawberries will not rise to the top of the sirup. Use only fresh, ripe, firm and sound berries. Prepare them, and add eight ounces of sugar and two tablespoonfuls of water to each quart of berries. Boil slowly for fifteen minutes in an enameled or acid-proof kettle. Allow the berries to cool and remain several hours or over-night in the covered kettle. Pack the cold berries in hot glass jars. Put rubbers and caps of jars in position, not tight. Sterilize for the length of time given below for the type of outfit used:

MINUTES Water bath, homemade or commercial 8 Water seal, 214 degrees 6 5 pounds steam pressure 5 10 pounds steam pressure. Do not use. Remove the jars, tighten the covers, invert the jars to cool and test the joints. Wrap the jars with paper to prevent bleaching.

CHAPTER III

HARD FRUITS

PINEAPPLES

The object of canning citrus fruits is, first, to save the surplus and by-products; second, to furnish wholesome fruits at reasonable cost to more of our people; third, to help the producer to transform by-products into net profits.

Almost every one likes canned pineapple, but some housewives stopped canning this fruit because they found that when cooked in sirup it seemed to get tough and less palatable. Vegetable and fruit fibers are toughened when cooked with sugar for any length of time, so in all cases where you desire to keep the product as Nature grew it avoid this form of cooking.

When the product is put into the jars with a sirup and cooked in the jar you will have a product superior to the one that is cooked over the direct fire in the kettle with the sirup.

But pineapple slices or pieces are so hard they cannot be put directly into the jars as berries are. Pineapples must undergo a preliminary process to make them palatable and soft. This preliminary process is known in canning as "blanching."

After the pineapple has been prepared by paring and removing the eyes, it can be left in slices or cut into cubes. In cutting hold the pineapple at the top and use a sharp knife. It is then placed in a wire basket or a piece of cheesecloth for the blanching. Blanching means to immerse the product in boiling water for a certain length of time to reduce its bulk and soften it.

Pineapples are blanched for five minutes. We scald peaches and apricots, which are soft fruits; but we blanch pineapples, apples and quinces, the hard fruits.

Scalding means to immerse the product in boiling water for a very short time—just long enough to loosen the skins. Blanching is just a longer period of scalding.

When you blanch pineapples use only enough water to cover them. This same blanching water can be used for making the sirup. It contains much of the pineapple flavor and there is no reason for discarding it. But this is absolutely the only blanching water that is ever used. All other blanching water, particularly that in which vegetables are blanched, is full of objectionable acids that we want to get rid of, so under no circumstances must it be used. But with pineapples the object of blanching is primarily to soften the hard fiber, so there is no objection to using the blanching water.

After the pineapple has been in the covered kettle of boiling water for five minutes, it is held under cold water until cool enough to handle. Never let it soak in cold water, as that will impair its delicate flavor. After this it is packed into hot sterilized jars. Rubber rings are put on the jars, the covers are put in place—not tight—and the jars are put in the canner.

Pineapple is sterilized for thirty minutes in a hot-water-bath outfit; thirty minutes in a condensed steam outfit; twenty-five minutes in the water-seal; twenty-five minutes in the steam pressure under five pounds of steam, and eighteen minutes in the pressure cooker under ten pounds of pressure. At the end of the sterilizing period the jars are removed, the covers completely tightened and the joints carefully tested for leakage.

A thin or medium-thin sirup is best for pineapples. Measure the blanching water and to every two cups of it add three cups of sugar. If you wish the sirup thin heat until the sugar is dissolved. If medium-thin sirup is desired, boil it about four minutes or until it begins to be sirupy.

STEPS IN CANNING PINEAPPLE

1. Cut the pineapple into slices of desired thickness.

2. Pare the slices. It is easier to pare the slices than to pare the whole pineapple.

3. Remove the eyes, using pineapple scissors to facilitate the work.

4. Blanch pineapple for five minutes in a small amount of boiling water, using a wire basket or cheesecloth.

5. Cold-dip the pineapple.

6. Make a sirup, using the blanching water. Make a thin or medium-thin sirup.

7. Pack the pineapple into hot sterilized jars,

with good rubbers on them.

8. Pour the sirup over the pineapple.

9. Put the tops of the jars on—not tight.

10. Sterilize for 30 minutes in hot-water-bath outfit, 30 minutes in condensed-steam outfit, 25 minutes in water-seal outfit, 25 minutes in steam pressure (5 pounds), 18 minutes in pressure cooker (10 pounds).

11. Remove from canner, tighten covers and inspect rubber and joints.

APPLES

Here are six ways in which canned apples may be used: as a breakfast dish, with cream and sugar; baked like fresh apples; in apple salad, often served for lunch or supper; as a relish with roast pork—the apples may be fried in the pork fat or the cores may be cooked with roast pork for flavoring; and for apple dumplings, deep apple pie and other desserts in which whole apples are desirable. The sirup of canned whole apples can be used for pudding sauces or fruit drinks.

Apples are another hard fruit which require blanching, as it greatly improves their texture and appearance.

Apples and some other fruits, such as pears and quinces, have a tendency to turn brown when allowed to stand after they are cut. To prevent their discoloring the pieces may be dropped into mild salt water as they are pared and sliced. Let them stand for five minutes, then wash them in clear water and pack. Use a thin sirup for canning apples.

Summer apples are not firm enough to keep

well when canned. They cook up and lose flavor.
They may, however, be canned to be used in a short
time. Windfall apples may be pared, cored and
sliced, using water, and only a small quantity of
that, instead of sirup, and canned for pies.

To be able to can windfall and cull apples
and thus have them for home use through the entire
year is a great advantage to all farmers who grow
them. They can be sold on the market canned when
they would not bring a cent in the fresh state.

The windfall and cull apples may be divided
into two grades. The first grade would include the
whole reasonably sound fruit; the second grade the
worm-eaten, partially decayed and injured fruit. Do
not can any injured or decayed part nor allow apples
to become overripe before canning.

Canning Whole Reasonably Firm Apples.
Wash the apples. Remove cores and blemishes.
Place whole apples in blanching tray or blanching
cloth and blanch in boiling hot water for one or two
minutes. Remove and plunge quickly into cold
water. Pack in large glass jars. Pour over the
product a hot thin sirup. Place rubber and top in
position. Seal partially—not tight.

Sterilize jars twenty minutes in hot-water-
bath outfit and in condensed steam, fifteen minutes
in water-seal, ten minutes in steam-pressure outfit
with five pounds of steam pressure, five minutes in
aluminum pressure-cooker outfit, under ten pounds
of steam pressure. Remove jars, tighten covers,
invert to cool and test joints.

Firm and tart apples may be cored and
peeled first, then canned by the above recipe.

Canning Apples for Pie Filling. Use second
grade of windfalls or culls. Wash, core, pare and

remove all decayed spots. Slice apple quickly into a basin containing slightly salted cold water—about one tablespoon of salt per gallon—to prevent discoloring. Pack fresh cold product in glass jars. Add one cupful of hot thin sirup to each quart of fruit. Put on the rubbers and screw on tops, but do not seal completely. Sterilize twelve minutes in hot-water bath or condensed-steam outfit; ten minutes in water-seal outfit; six minutes under five pounds of steam pressure; four minutes in aluminum pressure cooker. Remove jars, tighten covers, invert to cool and test joint. Store.

This filling can be used for making apple pies in the same way that fresh apples would be used, with the exception that the sirup must be poured off and less sugar should be used. Since the apples have already been cooked, only enough heat is needed to cook the crust and to warm the apples through. Pies may be baked in seven minutes. The apple pies made with these apples are, in the opinion of many housekeepers, as good as those made with fresh fruit, and they can be made in less time and are less expensive.

The only difference between canning apples for pies and salads or whole is that when wanted for pies the apples should be sliced immediately after placing in cold slightly salted water.

Canning Quartered Apples for Fruit Salads. Select best-grade culls of firm and rather tart varieties. Core, pare and quarter. Drop into basin containing slightly salted cold water. Pack these quartered pieces tightly in jars. Add a cup of hot thin sirup to each quart. Place rubber and top in position, partially seal—not tight. Sterilize twelve minutes in hot-water bath and condensed-steam outfits; ten minutes in water-seal outfit; six minutes under five pounds of steam pressure; four minutes in aluminum pressure cooker. Remove jars, tighten covers, invert to cool and test joints. Store.

ORANGES

Canning Whole Oranges and Other Citrus Fruits. Select windfall or packing-plant culls. Use no unsound or decayed fruit. Remove skin and white fiber on surface. Blanch fruit in boiling water one and a half minutes. Dip quickly in cold water. Pack containers full. Add boiling hot thin sirup. Place rubber and cap in position and partially seal— not tight.

Sterilize twelve minutes in hot-water-bath and condensed-steam outfits; eight minutes in water-seal outfit; six minutes in steam-pressure outfit under five pounds of steam; four minutes in aluminum pressure-cooker outfit. Remove jars, tighten covers, invert to cool and test joints. Wrap glass jars with paper to prevent bleaching, and store.

Canning Sliced Oranges for Salad Purposes. The oranges may be divided into their natural sections or sliced with a knife. Pack jars or containers full. Pour over product hot thin sirup. Place rubber and cap in position. Partially seal—not tight. Sterilize ten minutes in hot-water-bath and condensed-steam outfits; six minutes in water-seal outfit; five minutes in steam-pressure outfit with five pounds of steam; four minutes in aluminum pressure-cooker outfit under ten pounds of steam. Remove jars, tighten covers, invert to cool and test

the joints. Wrap jars with paper to prevent
bleaching, and store.

PEARS, QUINCES AND RHUBARB

Pears are prepared and canned just as the
whole firm apples are, being blanched a minute and
a half, cold-dipped and sterilized for the same
length of time as apples.

Quinces are so very hard they must be
blanched like pineapples, but for a longer time. Six
minutes' blanching is usually sufficient for quinces.
The sterilizing period can be determined by looking
at the chart.

If skins are left on rhubarb it keeps its pink
color. The hot dip is not necessary and may be
omitted. It removes some of the excessive acid in
the rhubarb which makes it objectionable to some
people. Be very careful not to hot-dip the rhubarb
more than one minute, for it gets mushy. An
advantage of the hot dip is that more rhubarb can be
packed in a jar after it has been hot-dipped.

WHAT A BUSHEL OF FRUIT WILL YIELD

A great many women have no conception of
how many jars of fruit they will get from a bushel or
half bushel of produce. It is wise to have a little
knowledge along this line, for it aids in planning the
winter's supply of canned goods as well as at
marketing time.

From one bushel of the various fruits you

will get on the average the following:
PRODUCTS, 1 BUSHEL PINT JARS QUART
JARS Windfall apples 30 20 Standard peaches 25
18 Pears 45 30 Plums 45 30 Berries 50 30 Windfall
oranges—sliced 22 15 Windfall oranges—whole 35
22

CANNING WITHOUT SUGAR

Though all instructions indicate that sugar is
necessary for the canning of all kinds of fruits, it is
not necessary for their proper sterilization and
preservation. Any fruit may be successfully
sterilized by simply adding boiling water instead of
the hot sirup. It is a well-known fact, however, that
most fruits canned in water will not retain so well
their natural flavor, texture and color as fruit canned
in sirup. When the product is to be used for pies,
salads, and so on it is not necessary to can in sirup.
When fruits canned in water are to be used for
sauces, the products should be sweetened before
use. In many instances it requires more sugar to
sweeten a sauce after canning than it does when the
product is canned in the hot sirup.
However, during the World War we had a
good chance to test the fruits which we canned
without sugar, when that commodity was scarce
and, in fact, impossible to get in very large
quantities. We used our fruits just as they were and
considered them very good. This all goes to show
that we can easily adjust ourselves to prevailing
conditions. In canning without the sugar sirup, you
would follow these directions:
Cull, stem or seed, and clean fruit by placing
in a strainer and pouring water over it until clean.

Pack product thoroughly in glass jars until full; use table knife or tablespoon for packing purposes. Pour over the fruit boiling water from kettle, place rubbers and caps in position, partially seal glass jars and place produce in canner.

If using hot-water-bath outfit sterilize from twenty to thirty minutes. After sterilizing remove packs, seal glass jars, wrap in paper to prevent bleaching, and store in a dry cool place.

When using a steam-pressure canner instead of the hot-water bath sterilize for ten minutes with five pounds of steam pressure. Never allow the pressure to go over ten pounds when you are canning soft fruits.

WHEN TO CAN

Inexperienced canners may not know when certain fruits are in season and at their prime for canning. The list below is necessarily subject to change, as seasons vary from year to year; but in normal years this table would hold true for the Northern States.

Apples September Apricots August Blackberries August Cherries July Currants July Gooseberries July Grapes September Huckleberries July Peaches August-September Pears September Pineapple June Plums August Quinces September Raspberries July Rhubarb All summer Strawberries May-June

For your canning you will need as your guide the charts on the pages which follow. They are very simple and will tell you how to prepare all the various fruits, whether or not they are to be blanched, and if so exactly how many minutes, and how long to cook or sterilize the products, according to the outfit you are using.

CHART FOR CANNING SOFT FRUITS AND BERRIES

NUMBER OF MINUTES TO STERILIZE KIND OF FRUIT / PREPARATION NUMBER OF MINUTES TO BLANCH OR HOT-DIP IN HOT WATER BATH OUTFIT AT 212°F IN CONDENSED STEAM OUTFIT IN WATER-SEAL OUTFIT 214°F IN STEAM PRESSURE 5 TO 10 POUNDS IN PRESSURE COOKER 10 POUNDS REMARKS APRICOTS: To remove skins hot-dip and cold-dip. Can be canned with the skins. Pits give a good flavor 1 to 2 16 16 12 10 5 Use medium-thick sirup BLACKBERRIES: Pick over, wash and stem None 16 16 12 10 5 Use medium-thin sirup BLUEBERRIES: Pick over, wash and stem None 16 16 12 10 5 Use medium-thin sirup CHERRIES: Wash, remove stems, and remove pits if desired. If pitted save the juice None 16 16 12 10 5 Use medium-thin sirup if sour; thin sirup if sweet CURRANTS: Wash and pick from stems None 16 16 12 10 5 Use medium-thin sirup CRANBERRIES: Wash and stem None 16 16 12 10 5 Use medium-thin sirup DEWBERRIES: Wash and stem None 16 16 12 10 5 Use medium-thin sirup FIGS: Wash and stem None 16 16 12 10 5 Figs can be hot- dipped for a minute or two if desired. Hot-dipping shrinks the figs so more can be packed in a jar GOOSEBERRIES Wash and snip off stems and blossom ends None 16 16 12 10 5

Use medium-thick sirup GRAPES Wash and pick from stems None 16 16 12 10 5 Use medium-thin sirup HUCKLEBERRIES Wash and stem None 16 16 12 10 5 Use medium-thin sirup PEACHES Blanch and cold-dip, then remove skins. 1-2 16 16 12 10 (Use only 5 pounds pressure.) X If peaches are canned under more than 5 pounds of pressure they become flavorless and dark in color PLUMS Wash; stones may be removed if desired. 1-2 16 16 12 10 5 For sweet plums use thin or medium-thin sirup; for sour plums use medium-thin sirup RASPBERRIES pick over, wash and stem None 16 16 12 10 5 Use medium-thin sirup RHUBARB Wash, cut into ½ inch pieces. Use sharp knife 1 16 16 12 10 5 Be very careful not to hot-dip the rhubarb more than one minute, for it gets mushy STRAWBERRIES Pick over, wash and hull None 16 16 12 10 5 Use medium-thick sirup HARD FRUITS APPLES Pare, core and cut into halves or smaller pieces 1½ to 2 20 20 15 10 5 Use thin sirup PEARS Wash, pare or not as desired. Small pears may be canned whole or quartered 1½ 20 20 15 10 5 Use thin sirup PINEAPPLE Cut into slices or inch cubes. The cores can be removed 5 30 30 25 25 18 Use thin or medium-thin sirup QUINCES Remove skins and cores. Cut into convenient slices 6 40 40 30 25 20 Apples, pears and quinces should be dropped into salt water to keep fruit from turning brown. Use salt in the proportion of one tablespoonful to one gallon of water. Use thin sirup WINDFALL APPLES FOR PIE FILLING Cut into halves None 12 12 10 6 4 Can in water QUARTERED APPLES FOR SALAD None 12 12 10 6 4 Can in water and save the sugar for other purposes CRAB APPLES Pare and core None 16 16

8 5 5 Can in water or use thin sirup CITRUS
FRUITS ORANGES, WHOLE Remove skins and
white fiber or surface, then blanch 1½ 12 12 8 6 4
Add boiling thin sirup LEMONS, WHOLE Remove
skins and white fiber or surface, then blanch 1½ 12
12 8 6 4 Add boiling thin sirup GRAPEFRUIT,
WHOLE Remove skins and white fiber or surface,
then blanch 1½ 12 12 8 6 4 Add boiling thin sirup
ORANGE AND OTHER CITRUS FRUITS,
SLICED Slice with a sharp knife None 10 10 6 5 4
Use thin sirup FRUITS CANNED IN WATER
WITHOUT SUGAR SIRUP 30 30 20 12 10
NOTE.—When cooking products in pint or half-
pint jars deduct three or four minutes from the time
given above. When cooking in two-quart jars add 3
or 4 minutes to time. The estimates given are for
quart jars.

CHAPTER IV

VEGETABLES

It is practical to can all vegetables, even
such difficult ones as corn, peas and beans, by the
cold-pack method of canning without using any
preservatives, if you will follow all directions,
instructions and the time-table accurately.
Vegetable canning is a little more complicated than
fruit canning.

TOMATOES

Every one likes canned tomatoes. In many homes more tomatoes are canned than any other product. The housewife uses them for soups, for sauces and for seasoning many meat dishes. Some women say: "I can preserve everything but tomatoes. They always spoil. What do I do wrong?" If the following directions are followed tomatoes will not spoil.

Tomatoes really are the easiest vegetable to can, because the period of sterilization is short, and many jars may be canned in a day, or if one is very busy a few jars may be canned daily without the expenditure of a great deal of time.

The best tomatoes for canning are those of moderate size, smooth and uniformly ripe. When a tomato ripens unevenly or when it is misshapen, it is difficult to peel, and the percentage of waste is high. Tomatoes should not be picked when they are green or partly ripe, for the flavor will not be so good as when they are allowed to remain upon the vines until fully ripe. Care should be taken, however, not to allow them to become overripe before canning.

In no instance should a tomato with a rotten spot be canned, even though the spot is cut out, for the occasional spoiled jar resulting from this attempted saving will cost more than the partly spoiled tomatoes are worth. If the housewife will can only uniformly ripe, sound tomatoes, saving the small, uneven but sound fruit for tomato *purée*, she will have a much better-looking pack and greater food value at the close of the season. Yellow tomatoes may be canned in the same manner as are the more common red varieties, except that it is not necessary to remove the cores.

First of all, grade for ripeness, size and quality; this is to insure a high-grade product. We could, of course, can different sizes and shades together, but uniform products are more pleasing to the eye and will sterilize much more evenly. If the products are of the same ripeness and quality, the entire pack will receive the proper degree of cooking.

Wash the tomatoes. Have ready a kettle of boiling water. Put the tomatoes in a wire basket, or lay them on a piece of cheesecloth or a towel, twist the ends together to form a sack, and let this down into the kettle. It is a good plan to slip a rubber band round the neck of this sack to hold the ends in place. The ends should be long enough to stand up out of the water and so avoid danger of burning the fingers when removing the product.

Have the water boiling hard. Lower the tomatoes into the boiling water. This is called scalding the tomatoes. We scald the tomatoes to loosen the skin. If the tomatoes are very ripe, one minute scalding will be sufficient. The average length of time for tomatoes, just perfect for canning, is one and a half minutes. Do not leave the tomatoes in the hot water until the skins break, as this gives them a fuzzy appearance.

The scalding kettle always should be covered, to keep in all the heat possible. Begin to time from the minute the product is immersed in the boiling water. If you wait until the water comes back to a boil, you will scald the product too long and have mushy tomatoes.

Lift the tomatoes out of the hot water and

plunge them immediately into cold water, or hold them under the cold-water faucet. The cold-dip makes them easier to handle, separates the skin from the pulp, firms the texture, and coagulates the coloring matter so it stays near the surface, giving them a rich, red color. Then the shock due to the sudden change from hot to cold and back to hot again seems to help kill the spores. Do not let the product stand in the cold-dip. The water becomes lukewarm, softens the product and allows bacteria to develop.

Take the tomato in the left hand and with a sharp knife cut out the core. Be careful not to cut into the fleshy portion or seed cells, for this will scatter the seeds and pulp through the liquid, injuring the appearance of the product. Cut out the core before removing the skin, for the skin will protect the pulp and there will be less danger of breaking the tomato. If the tomatoes are ripe and have been scalded properly, the skin can be slipped off with the fingers.

The jars, rubbers and tops should be ready. Glass jars should be hot, so there will be no danger of breakage in setting them in the hot water, and so they will not cool the water in the cooker below the boiling point.

Pack the tomatoes whole, pressing and shaking them well down together, but not using force enough to crush them.

Now we come to a point where tomatoes are different from most vegetables. Beans, carrots, peas, and so on, have hot water added to them. But as a large part of the tomato is water, no more is needed. Another exception where no water is needed is with the "greens family." So with tomatoes we add no water, but add one teaspoonful of salt and one teaspoonful of sugar, just for seasoning, to every quart jar. I think that tomatoes always are improved by the addition of a little sugar, but this is not necessary and can be omitted, as also can be the salt.

The salt in canning does not act as a preservative, but as seasoning; so if for any reason you forget the salt, do not be alarmed. Your products will keep perfectly without the salt.

THE WAY TO SEAL

The products are in the hot jars now. The jars do not need to be full in order to keep. If you were canning by the "open-kettle" method, the air in the partly filled jar would not have been sterilized, and might contain the bacteria which cause the product to ferment or mold. But by the cold pack, the air in the can is sterilized while the product is being sterilized; and if the can is closed immediately after cooking, a single spoonful may be canned in a two-quart jar and the product will keep indefinitely.

Place Rubber and Cover on Jar. Fit the rubber. Use good rubbers and see that they lie flat and fit close up to the can. Put the covers in place.

Do Not Seal Glass Jars Tight. If using screw-top jars screw each cover down until it catches, then turn a quarter of a round back; or screw down with the thumb and little finger, not using force but stopping when the cover catches.

If using vacuum-seal jars put the cover on and the spring in place. The spring will give enough to allow the steam to escape.

If using glass-top jars, with the patent wire snap, put the cover in place, the wire over the top and the clamp up.

The cover on a glass jar must not be tight while processing, because the air will expand when heated, and if the cover is not loose enough to allow the steam to escape, the pressure may blow the rubber out or break the jar.

When canning in tin we cap and tip the cans at once. The tin will bulge out, but is strong enough to withstand the pressure, and when the contents cool the can will come back into shape.

The jars are now ready for the canner. Tomatoes sterilized under boiling water require twenty-two minutes; in condensed-steam cooker, twenty-two minutes; in water-seal, eighteen minutes; in steam-pressure, with five pounds, fifteen minutes, and in the pressure cooker, at ten or fifteen pounds, ten minutes.

If you use the homemade outfit or any water-bath outfit be sure the water is boiling when the jars of tomatoes are lowered into the canner. Time lost in bringing the contents to the point of sterilization softens the tomatoes and results in inferior goods. Use the ordinary good sense with which you have been endowed in handling the jars and you will have no breakage. At the end of the sterilizing period, remove the jars.

In taking canned goods from boiling hot water, care is needed to see that they are protected from drafts. If necessary close the windows and doors while lifting the jars out, for a sudden draft might break them.

Examine rubbers to see that they are in

place. Sometimes, if the covers are screwed down too tight, the pressure of the steam from the inside causes the rubber to bulge out. Simply loosen the cover a thread or two, push the rubber back into place and then tighten. In case the rubber does not seem to fit well or seems to be a poor rubber, it should be replaced by a new one and the jar returned to the cooker for five minutes.

The jars should be sealed tight—covers screwed down, clamps put in place—immediately after they are removed from the cooker.

Invert to test the joint and cool. If the seal is not perfect, correct the fault, and return the jar to the cooker for five minutes if hot, ten minutes if jar is cold.

Do not invert vacuum-seal jars. These should be allowed to cool and then tested by removing the spring or clamp and lifting the jars by the cover only. Lift the jar only a half inch, holding it over the table so that, in case the lid does not hold, the jar and contents will not be damaged. Or, better still, tap round the edge of the cover with a ruler. An imperfect seal will cause a hollow sound.

Tomato Purée. Small, misshapen, unevenly ripened tomatoes may be converted into tomato *purée*. The tomatoes should be washed, run through a colander to remove skins and cores, concentrated by cooking to about half the original volume, and packed in the jars. Rubbers and tops should then be placed in position and the product sterilized for the same length of time as for canned tomatoes. *Purée* even may be kept in bottles sealed with sterilized corks and dipped several times in paraffin.

HOW OTHER VEGETABLES ARE CANNED

All other vegetables are canned exactly like tomatoes, with two exceptions. Tomatoes are scalded. All other vegetables are blanched. We scald tomatoes to loosen the skins and to start the flow of the coloring matter, which is later arrested or coagulated by the cold-dip.

Blanching is scalding, only for a longer time. Scalding is never for more than two minutes. Blanching covers from three to thirty minutes.

We blanch beans, peas, corn, cabbage, carrots, beets, turnips, and so on, for three to ten minutes. We blanch these vegetables to eliminate any objectionable acids or bitter flavors which may be present, and thus improve the flavor; to reduce the bulk so we can pack closer; to start the flow of the coloring matter; to improve the texture of the vegetables by making them more tender, and to improve the appearance by helping to make clear the liquid in the jar. Blanching is what makes for success in the cold-pack method of canning. Blanching is *very* important and must be carefully and accurately done.

Let me repeat about blanching: Have the kettle of blanching water *boiling vigorously, completely immerse* the product in the boiling water, cover the kettle *immediately* and begin to time the product. Do not stand with the cover in hand and wait for the water to come back to the boil, for, of course, it stopped boiling for a second when you lowered into it the cold product. If you cover the kettle the water will quickly reboil. Do not keep wondering if it is boiling and take off the cover to see. All these may seem foolish precautions, but it is necessary to follow directions accurately.

And remember, all things that are scalded or blanched must be followed immediately by a cold plunge or "cold-dip." The scalding or blanching is the "hot-dip," and this must be followed by the "cold-dip." You may be asking, what is the point of this "cold-dip"? It is a very logical question.

We "cold-dip" a product to harden the pulp under the skin and thus permit the removal of the skin without injury to the pulp; to coagulate the coloring matter and make it harder to dissolve during the sterilization period and to make it easier to handle the products in packing, and to subject the product to a sudden shock by quick change in temperature.

STEPS IN CANNING VEGETABLES

If you will follow these steps for all vegetable canning you cannot help but be successful:

1. Clean jars and test rubbers. If rubbers do not return to normal shape after stretching, do not use.

2. Prepare material to be canned, according to directions given on chart.

3. Hot-dip—blanch or scald—the prepared food. This process consists of immersing the prepared product in boiling water for different lengths of time, according to the material to be canned. See chart. Hot-dipping shrinks the product and enables one to pack more material in a jar.

4. Cold-dip the material. This process consists of plunging the blanched or scalded food into cold water, which makes it more easily handled. Be sure the water is cold; the colder the better.

Take the product out immediately and let it drain. *Don't let any food soak in the cold water.*

From this point on, speed is highly important. The blanched vegetables which are slightly warm must not be allowed to remain out of the jars a moment longer than is necessary.

Remove skins when required, and as each article is pared cut it into pieces of proper size and

5. Pack directly into the clean, scalded cans or jars. Pack as solidly as possible, being careful not to bruise or mash soft products. Pack the product to within three-eighths of an inch of the top. Lima beans, navy beans, peas, corn, pumpkin and sweet potatoes swell, so pack them within only one inch of the top of the jar.

6. Add seasoning. One teaspoonful salt to every quart jar of vegetables, and an equal amount of sugar to tomatoes, corn and peas if desired.

7. Add boiling water to within a quarter inch of top to all vegetables, except tomatoes and greens. Tomatoes contain ninety-four per cent water, so none should be added. Tomato juice can be used if desired. Greens are canned in just the water that clings to the leaves after the cold-dip.

8. Adjust rubber rings and the covers of the jars; partially seal.

9. Sterilize—see time-table on pages following.

10. Remove from canner and completely seal. Test for leaks. Cool jars as rapidly as possible,

without drafts striking them.

Rapid cooling of the product prevents overcooking, clarifies the liquid and preserves the shape and texture of the product.

SPECIAL DIRECTIONS FOR VARIOUS VEGETABLES

Greens. No water is added to greens. Ninety percent of greens is water. They are high in mineral matter and we must preserve that.

Asparagus. Remove string before packing in jar. Can or dry tough ends for soup. If asparagus is packed in jars as whole stalks, pack with the tips up.

Tomatoes. Remove skins before packing. Tomatoes may be canned whole or in pieces. Skin, cook and strain imperfect tomatoes. Use this for liquid; as 94 per cent of the tomato is water, no water is needed.

Eggplants. Make slices about ½ to ¾ of an inch thick. Do not add salt, as it causes eggplants to turn dark.

Pumpkin and squash. If you do not wish to scrape out of the shells you can remove seeds, pare and cut into small blocks of uniform size. Then blanch.

Sweet corn. Corn expands a little in processing, and for this reason jars should not be filled quite full. Corn that has reached the dough stage before being packed will have a cheesy appearance after canning. Corn should never be allowed to remain in the cold-dip water.

Field corn. This product is commonly

known as corn-club breakfast food. The corn should be selected between the milk and the dough stage. Wide-mouthed glass jars or tin cans should be used for canning this product. Avoid packing container too full, as the product swells during the sterilization period. The corn should be canned the same day it is picked from the field if possible. After this product has been sterilized and cooked and stored away it will form a solid, butter-like mass which may be cut into convenient slices for toasting, frying and baking purposes.

Mushrooms. Do not fail to blanch and cold dip. After opening containers remove the mushrooms immediately and use them as quickly as possible.

Sweet peppers. Place the peppers in the oven and bake them until the skins separate from the meat. Remove the skin. Pack in hot jars. Add 1 teaspoonful of salt to a quart. Add boiling water.

Lima beans. Lima beans can be either blanched or steamed. If blanched allow 5 minutes; if in live steam allow 10.

Wax or string beans. Beans can be canned whole or cut into uniform pieces.

Cabbage and cauliflower. Cabbage and cauliflower should be soaked in cold brine (½ lb. salt to 12 quarts water) for one hour before blanching.

Brussels sprouts. Use small solid heads.

Peas. A cloudy or hazy appearance of the liquid indicates that the product was roughly handled in blanching and cold dipping, or that broken peas were not removed before packing.

Carrots and parsnips. Carrots can be packed whole, in slices or in cross-section pieces. Skin of parsnips can be scraped off after blanching and cold dipping.

Beets. Small beets that run 40 to a quart are the most suitable size for first-class packs. Well-canned beets will show a slight loss of color when removed from the canner, but will brighten up in a few days.

Turnips. Scrape skin after blanching and cold dipping.

Corn and tomatoes. Add 1 teaspoonful of salt to every quart of mixture. Mix 2 parts of tomatoes with 1 part corn. One teaspoonful of sugar improves the flavor.

Corn, tomatoes and string beans. Use 1 part of corn, 1 part of green string beans and 3 parts of tomatoes. Add 1 teaspoonful of salt and 1 teaspoonful of sugar to every quart jar.

CHARTS FOR CANNING ALL VEGETABLES AND GREENS
NUMBER OF MINUTES TO STERILIZE VEGETABLES / PREPARATION SCALDING OR BLANCHING MINUTES IN BOILING WATER OR HOMEMADE OUTFIT (212°F.) IN CONDENSED STEAM OUTFIT IN WATER-SEAL OUTFIT 214°F IN STEAM PRESSURE 5 TO 10 POUNDS IN PRESSURE COOKER 10 POUNDS *Class 1—Greens, Domestic and Wild* ALL GREENS—SPINACH, BEET TOPS, CHARD, DANDELIONS, ETC. Pick over; wash in several waters. Steam in colander or in steamer until wilted Takes about 15 minutes. 120 (2 hr) 120 (2 hr) 90 (1½ hr) 60 (1 hr) 40, at 10 lbs. *Class 2 — Special Vegetables* ASPARAGUS Wash, remove woody ends; cut to fit jar; tie in bundles. Blanch tough ends 4 minutes, tip ends 2 minutes. 90 (1½

hr) 90 (1½ hr) 60 (1 hr) 50 25, at 10 lbs.
TOMATOES Select fresh, ripe, firm tomatoes.
Skins will slip off after scalding and cold dipping.
Scald 1½ 22 22 18 18 10, at 10 lbs. EGGPLANTS
Remove skin after blanching and cold dipping.
Slice crosswise and pack. Blanch 3 60 (1 hr) 60 (1
hr) 50 45 30, at 10 lbs. PUMPKIN AND SQUASH
Cut into sections; remove seeds; scrape shells after
blanching and cold dipping. Blanch 5 120 (2 hr)
120 (2 hr) 90 (1½ hr) 60 (1 hr) 40, at 10 lbs.
CORN—SWEET Cut corn from cob, blanch
immediately after and cold dip. 5 on cob 180 (3 hr)
180 (3 hr) 120 (2 hr) 90 (1½ hr) 60, at 10 lbs.
CORN—FIELD Remove husk and silk. Cut the
corn from the cob after it has been blanched and
cold dipped. Feed the corn to a food chopper and
grind to a pulp. Cook this product in a kettle, add ⅔
teaspoonful sugar and ⅓ teaspoonful salt to each
quart. Cook (stir while cooking) until the product
has assumed a thickened or pastelike mass. 10 180
(3 hr) 180 (3 hr) 120 (2 hr) 60 (1 hr) 50, at 10 lbs.
MUSHROOMS If small, can them whole; if large
they may be cut into sections. 5 90 (1½ hr) 90 (1½
hr) 80 (1⅓ hr) 50 30, at 10 lbs. SWEET PEPPERS
Use either green or red peppers. .. 90 (1½ hr) 90
(1½ hr) 75 (1¾ hr) 60 (1 hr) 40, at 10 lbs. *Class 3—
Pod Vegetables and Other Green Products*
BEANS—LIMA Shell and wash. 5 to 10 180 (3 hr)
180 (3 hr) 120 (2 hr) 60 (1 hr) 40, at 10 lbs.
BEANS—WAX OR STRING Wash and string. 5 to
10 120 (2 hr) 120 (2 hr) 90 (1½ hr) 60 (1 hr) 40, at
10 lbs. CABBAGE Use small solid heads of
cabbage. 5 to 10 120 (2 hr) 120 (2 hr) 90 (1½ hr) 60
(1 hr) 40, at 10 lbs. CAULIFLOWER Use flowered
portion of cauliflower. 3 60 (1 hr) 60 (1 hr) 40 30

20, at 15 lbs. BRUSSELS SPROUTS Cut into sections and remove core. 5 to 10 120 (2 hr) 120 (2 hr) 90 (1½ hr) 60 (1 hr) 40, at 10 lbs. PEAS Shell and wash. Add 1 teaspoonful of salt and 1 teaspoonful of sugar toevery quart. 5 to 10 180 (3 hr) 180 (3 hr) 120 (2 hr) 60 (1 hr) 40, at 10 to 15 lbs. *Class 4—Roots and Tuber Vegetables* CARROTS, PARSNIPS, SALSIFY Remove skin by scraping after blanching and cold dipping. 5 90 (1½ hr) 90 (1½ hr) 80 (1⅓ hr) 60 (1 hr) 40, at 10 lbs. BEETS To retain the color of beets leave 3 or 4 inches of the stem and all the root on while blanching. After cold dipping, the skin may be removed Scrape the skin. 5 90 (1½ hr) 90 (1½ hr) 80 (1⅓ hr) 60 (1 hr) 40, at 10 lbs. TURNIPS Wash thoroughly with a vegetable brush. 5 90 (1½ hr) 90 (1½ hr) 80 (1⅓ hr) 60 (1 hr) 40, at 10 lbs. *Class 5—Vegetable Combinations* CORN AND TOMATOES Prepare individual vegetables and then combine and pack. .. 120 (2 hr) 120 (2 hr) 120 (2 hr) 60 (1 hr) 45, at 10 lbs. CORN,

TOMATOES AND
STRING BEANS 3
1½
5 120 (2 hr) 120 (2 hr) 120 (2 hr) 60 (1 hr) 45, at 10 lbs. Count from time when water begins to boil (bubbles all over). This time schedule is for both pint and quart jars. Add 30 minutes to time of sterilizing for 2-quart jars.

CHAPTER V

SOUPS

After one has learned how to can fruits and vegetables successfully, the next thing to attempt is the canning of soups.

Soups may be canned with or without meat. We make one variety which is a pure vegetable soup. We use no stock or meat, and can it in its own juice or liquor, thus using no water.

When we wish to use it we dilute it three or four times and serve it as a vegetable soup or, more frequently, when we have chicken bones or any meat bones on hand, we add a can of this concentrated vegetable mixture to the bones and make a delicious stock soup.

I will give this recipe as I have given it to many friends, all of whom have pronounced it excellent:

1 Peck ripe tomatoes
1 Head cabbage
1 Dozen carrots
1 White turnip
3 Pounds string beans
1 Pound okra
3 Red peppers
1 Peck spinach
2 Pounds asparagus
6 Small beets
6 Ears sweet corn

Scald the tomatoes by placing them in a wire basket and plunging them into boiling water for one and a half minutes. Cold-dip them immediately. After removing the core and stem end of the tomato, the skin slips right off. Save all the tomato juice. Cut the tomatoes into quarters. Put into a large pail or bucket with the juice. Blanch the cabbage, carrots, turnip, string beans, okra and sweet red peppers five minutes. Cold-dip. Of course you blanch and cold-dip each product separately. Cut each vegetable after it is blanched and cold-dipped into small cubes and add to the tomatoes.

Spinach must be carefully washed to remove all grit and sand. All greens must be washed through several waters to cleanse them thoroughly.

Instead of blanching the spinach in a kettle of boiling water, as we do the other vegetables, we steam it by placing it in a colander over boiling water or in a regulation steamer with tightly fitting cover, such as is used for steaming suet puddings and brown bread. If you can with a steam-pressure canner or a pressure cooker, then steam the spinach there. If we boiled the spinach for fifteen or twenty minutes we would lose a quantity of the mineral salts, the very thing we aim to get into our systems when we eat spinach, dandelion greens, Swiss chard and other greens. After the blanching or steaming comes the cold dip.

There is something about blanching asparagus, either for soups or when canned alone, that is worth knowing. Instead of blanching the whole stalk of asparagus for the same length of time, we use a little discretion, giving the tougher, harder ends a full four minutes' blanching, but allowing the tender tip ends only two minutes. You are possibly wondering how that is done.

Tie the asparagus stalks in bunches and put

the bunches with all the tips standing one way on a piece of cheesecloth. Tie the cloth or snap rubber bands round it, and then stand the asparagus in boiling water in an upright position for two minutes; next lay the asparagus lengthwise in the blanching water for another two minutes, and you have accomplished your purpose. You have given the tougher parts two minutes' more blanching than the tender parts. Use a deep enough kettle so the asparagus will be completely covered when laid lengthwise. After the blanching, cold-dip the asparagus.

Wash the beets. Leave two inches of the top and all the tail on the beets while blanching. Blanch for five minutes, then cold-dip. Next scrape off the skin, top and tail. The tops can be put right into the soup too. Any surplus tops can be steamed with the spinach and can be treated similarly.

Blanch corn on the cob five minutes. Cold-dip. Cut the corn from the cob, cutting from tip to butt end. Add the corn to the other vegetables. Add no water. Pack the mixed vegetables into clean glass jars; add one level teaspoonful of salt to every jar; partially seal; cook one hour and a half in wash-boiler or other homemade outfit. At the end of that period remove jars from canner, seal tight, and the work is done.

Of course you are interested in the cost of this soup. Most of the ingredients came right from our garden. We had to buy the okra and the red peppers, but I figured everything just as if I had to buy it from the market; and on this basis, the cost of our soup would have been only seven and a half cents a can. We canned it in tin, using size Number Two, which is the same as pint size in glass jars.

Another vegetable soup without stock, dried beans and peas being used, is made as follows:

Soak six pounds of Lima beans and four pounds of dry peas over night. Boil each thirty minutes. Blanch sixteen pounds of carrots, six pounds of cabbage, three pounds of celery, six pounds of turnips, four pounds of okra, one pound of onions, and four pounds of parsley for three minutes and dip in cold water quickly. Prepare the vegetables and chop into small cubes. Chop the onions and celery extra fine. Mix all of them thoroughly and season to taste. Pack in glass jars or tin cans. Fill with boiling water. Partially seal glass jars. Cap and tip tin cans. Process ninety minutes if using hot-water-bath outfit or condensed-steam outfit; sixty minutes if using water-seal outfit or five-pound steam-pressure outfit; forty-five minutes if using pressure cooker.

In many homes cream of tomato soup is the favorite. To make this soup the housewife uses a tomato pulp and combines it with milk and seasonings. You can can a large number of jars of this pulp and have it ready for the cream soup. To make and can this pulp follow these directions:

Tomato Pulp. Place the tomatoes in a wire basket or piece of cheesecloth and plunge into boiling water for one and a half minutes. Plunge into cold water. Remove the skins and cores. Place the tomatoes in a kettle and boil thirty minutes. Pass the tomato pulp through a sieve. Pack in glass jars while hot and add a level teaspoonful of salt per quart. Partially seal glass jars. Sterilize twenty minutes if using hot-water-bath outfit or condensed-steam outfit; eighteen minutes if using water-seal, or five-pound steam-pressure outfit; fifteen minutes if using pressure-cooker outfit.

Soup Stock. To make the soup stock which is the foundation of all the stock soups, use this recipe:

Secure twenty-five pounds of beef hocks, joints and bones containing marrow. Strip off the fat and meat and crack bones with hatchet or cleaver. Put the broken bones in a thin cloth sack and place this in a large kettle containing five gallons of cold water. Simmer—do not boil—for six or seven hours. Do not salt while simmering. Skim off all fat. This should make about five gallons of stock. Pack hot in glass jars, bottles or enameled or lacquered tin cans. Partially seal glass jars. Cap and tip tin cans. Sterilize forty minutes if using hot-water-bath outfit or condensed-steam outfit; thirty minutes if using water-seal or five-pound steam-pressure outfit; twenty-five minutes if using pressure-cooker outfit.

Soups made with soup stock are many and varied. One can utilize the things at hand and change the distinctive flavor from year to year. I will give you a few good specimen recipes which if followed will give good results:

Vegetable Soup. Soak a quarter pound dried Lima beans and one pound unpolished rice for twelve hours. Cook a half pound pearl barley for two hours. Blanch one pound carrots, one pound onions, one medium-size potato and one red pepper for three minutes and cold-dip. Prepare the vegetables and cut into small cubes. Mix thoroughly Lima beans, rice, barley, carrots, onions, potato and red pepper. Fill glass jars or the enameled tin cans three-fourths full of the above mixture of vegetables and cereals. Make a smooth paste of a half pound of wheat flour and blend in five gallons soup stock. Boil three minutes and add four ounces salt. Pour this stock over vegetables and fill cans. Partially seal glass jars. Cap and tip tin cans. Sterilize ninety minutes if using hot-water-bath outfit or condensed-steam outfit; seventy-five minutes if using a water-seal or five-pound steam-pressure outfit; forty-five minutes if using pressure-cooker outfit.

Cream of Pea Soup. Soak eight pounds of dried peas over night. Cook until soft. Mash fine. Add the mashed peas to five gallons of soup stock and bring to boil. Pass the boiling liquid through a fine sieve. Make a smooth paste of a half pound flour and add paste, ten ounces of sugar and three ounces of salt to the soup stock. Cook until soup begins to thicken. Pack in glass jars or tin cans. Partially seal glass jars. Cap and tip tin cans. Process ninety minutes if using hot-water-bath outfit or condensed-steam outfit; eighty minutes if using water-seal outfit; seventy minutes if using five-pound steam-pressure outfit; forty-five minutes if using pressure-cooker outfit.

Cream of Potato Soup. Boil one and a half pounds of potatoes, sliced thin, and five gallons of soup stock for ten minutes. Add three ounces of salt, a quarter teaspoonful of pepper and a half pound of butter and boil slowly for five minutes. Make three tablespoonfuls of flour into smooth paste and add to the above. Cook three minutes and pack in glass jars or tin cans while hot. Partially seal glass jars. Cap and tip tin cans. Sterilize ninety minutes if using a hot-water-bath outfit or condensed-steam outfit; seventy-five minutes if using a water-seal outfit; sixty-five minutes if using a five-pound steam-pressure outfit; forty-five minutes if using a pressure-cooker outfit.

Bean Soup. Soak three pounds of dried beans twelve hours in cold water. Cut two pounds of ham into quarter-inch cubes and place in a small sack. Place beans, ham and four gallons of water in kettle and boil slowly until the beans are very soft. Remove the ham and beans from the liquor and mash the beans fine. Return ham and mashed beans to the liquor, add five gallons of soup stock and seasoning, and bring to boil. Pack into jars or cans while hot. Partially seal jars. Cap and tip tin cans. Process two hours if using hot-water-bath or condensed-steam outfit; ninety minutes if using water-seal outfit; seventy-five minutes if using five-pound steam-pressure outfit; sixty minutes if using pressure cooker.

Okra Soup. Slice eight pounds okra into thin slices the round way. Blanch ten minutes and cold-dip. Boil one and a half pounds rice for twenty-five minutes. Mix okra and rice and fill cans or jars half full. To five gallons soup stock add five ounces salt, a quarter teaspoonful of coriander seed and a quarter teaspoonful of powdered cloves, and bring to boil. Fill remaining portion of jars or cans. Partially seal glass jars. Cap and tip tin cans. Process two hours if using hot-water-bath outfit or condensed-steam outfit; ninety minutes if using water-seal outfit; seventy-five minutes if using five-pound steam-pressure outfit; sixty minutes if using pressure-cooker outfit.

Chicken-Soup Stock. Place thirty pounds chicken in ten gallons of cold water and simmer for five hours. Remove meat and bones, then strain. Add sufficient water to make ten gallons of stock. Fill glass jars or tin cans with hot stock. Partially seal glass jars. Cap and tip tin cans. This stock is used to make soup where the term "chicken-soup stock" is used. Process ninety minutes if using hot-water-bath outfit or condensed-steam outfit; seventy-five minutes if using water-seal outfit; sixty minutes if using five-pound steam-pressure outfit; forty-five minutes if using pressure-cooker outfit.

Chicken Broth With Rice. For each gallon of soup stock use twelve ounces of rice. Boil rice thirty minutes. Fill jars or tin cans two-thirds full of rice and the remainder with soup stock. Partially seal glass jars. Cap and tip tin cans. Process ninety minutes if using hot-water-bath outfit or condensed-steam outfit; seventy-five minutes if using water-seal outfit; sixty minutes if using five-pound steam-pressure outfit; forty-five minutes if using pressure-cooker outfit.

Chicken Gumbo. Cut two pounds ham into small cubes and boil thirty minutes. Mince three pounds chicken and chop half a pound of onions fine. Make a smooth paste of a half pound flour. Add above to five gallons of chicken-soup stock. Then add a half pound butter and a quarter pound salt and boil ten minutes. Next add three ounces powdered okra mixed with one pint water. Pack into glass jars or tin cans while hot. Partially seal glass jars. Cap and tip tin cans. Process ninety minutes if using hot-water-bath outfit or condensed-steam outfit; seventy-five minutes if using water-seal outfit; sixty minutes if using five-pound steam-pressure outfit; forty-five minutes if using pressure-cooker outfit.

TOMATO ACID CHECKS BACTERIA

Some women who have canned soup tell me it spoiled or tasted "sourish and smelled sourish too." This is what we call "flat sour." It may happen to any vegetable you can, as well as to the soups. "Flat sour" affects peas, beans, asparagus and corn more than other vegetables. If the vegetables have been picked for some time and the bacteria have had a chance "to work," and you are not exceedingly careful about your canning, you may develop "flat sour" in the soup. If you let one little spore of this bacteria survive all is lost. Its moist growing place is favorable to development, particularly if not much acid is present. One little spore left in a jar will multiply in twenty hours to some twenty millions of bacteria. This twenty million can stand on the point of a needle, so a can could acquire quite a large population in a short time. Bacteria do not like acids, so it is always a good idea to have tomatoes in your soup mixture, and get the tomatoes into the stone crock early in the game. The tomato acid will safeguard the other vegetables which lack acid.

If you are careless about the blanching and cold-dipping—that is, not doing these full time—if you work too slowly in getting the products into jars and then let the full jars stand in the warm atmosphere, you are pretty sure to develop "flat sour."

Place each jar in the canner as it is packed. The first jars in will not be affected by the extra cooking. Have the water just below the boiling point as you put in each jar. When you have the canner full bring the water to the boiling point as quickly as possible and begin to count cooking or sterilizing time from the moment it does boil.

Some women make the mistake at the end of the cooking period of letting the jars remain in the boiling water, standing on the false bottom of the canner until they are cool enough to handle with no danger of burning the hands. This slow method of cooling not only tends to create "flat sour," but it is apt to result in cloudy-looking jars and in mushy vegetables.

For this reason you should have in your equipment a lifter with which you can lift out the hot jars without the hands touching them. If you use a rack with wire handles this answers the same purpose.

This "flat sour," which is not at all dangerous from the standpoint of health, must not be confused with the botulinus bacteria, which is an entirely different thing.

"Flat sour," perfectly harmless, appears often with inexperienced canners. Botulinus, harmful, appears rarely. You need not be at all alarmed about eating either "flat sour" or botulinus, because the odor from spoiled goods is so distasteful—it really resembles rancid cheese—that you would never get a spoon of it to your mouth.

If you are debating whether this jar or that jar of soup or vegetables is spoiled, do not *taste* the contents of the jar. *Smell* it. Tasting might poison you if you happened on the botulinus bacteria, which is so rare it need alarm no one; whereas smelling is perfectly safe.

TIME-TABLE FOR SOUPS

GRAY SOUP WITHOUT STOCK

INGREDIENTS NUMBER OF
MINUTES
TO BLANCH OTHER PREPARATION 1 Peck
ripe tomatoes Scald 1½ Remove core and stem end.
1 Head cabbage
1 Dozen carrots
1 White turnip
2 Pounds string beans
1 Pound okra
3 Red peppers 5
5
5
5
5
5 Cut into cubes after blanching 1 Peck spinach ..
Steam 15 minutes or until thoroughly wilted. 2
Pounds asparagus 4 Cut into small pieces after
blanching. 6 Small beets 5 Cut into slices after
blanching. 6 Ears sweet corn 5 Cut from cob after
blanching. Salt .. NUMBER OF MINUTES TO
STERILIZE

In boiling water or homemade outfit, 212
degrees Fahrenheit, 90.
In condensed steam outfit, 90.
In water-seal outfit, 214 degrees Fahrenheit,
60.
In steam-pressure outfit, 5 pounds, 60.
In pressure-cooker outfit, 10 to 15 pounds,
45.

VEGETABLE SOUP WITHOUT STOCK, USING DRY LEGUMES

INGREDIENTS NUMBER OF
MINUTES
TO BLANCH OTHER PREPARATION 6 Pounds
dried Lima beans
4 Pounds dried peas Soak over night, then boil
for one half hour. 16 Pounds carrots
6 Pounds cabbage
3 Pounds celery
6 Pounds turnips 3
3
3
3 Cut into small cubes after blanching. 4 Pounds
okra 3 Cut into slices after blanching. 1 Pound
onions 3 Chop fine after blanching. 4 Pounds
parsley Salt 3 Cut into pieces after blanching.
NUMBER OF MINUTES TO STERILIZE

In boiling water or homemade outfit, 212
degrees Fahrenheit, 90.
In condensed steam outfit, 90.
In water-seal outfit, 214 degrees Fahrenheit,
60.
In steam-pressure outfit, 5 pounds, 60.
In pressure-cooker outfit, 10 to 15 pounds,
45.

SOUP STOCK (Foundation of All Stock Soups)

25 Pounds beef hocks, joints and bones Simmer for 6 or 7 hours. 5 Gallons water Should make 5 Gallons stock. NUMBER OF MINUTES TO STERILIZE

In boiling water or homemade outfit, 212 degrees Fahrenheit, 40.

In condensed steam outfit, 40.

In water-seal outfit, 214 degrees Fahrenheit, 30.

In steam-pressure outfit, 5 pounds, 30.

In pressure-cooker outfit, 10 to 15 pounds, 25.

VEGETABLE SOUP WITH STOCK

INGREDIENTS NUMBER OF MINUTES
TO BLANCH OTHER PREPARATION ¼ Pounds dried Lima beans Soak 12 hours. 1 Pound rice Soak 12 hours. ¼ Pound pearl barley Cook 2 hours.

1 Pounds carrots

1 Pounds onions

1 Potato

1 Red Pepper 3

3

3

3 Cut into small cubes after blanching. ½ Pound flour

5 Gallons soup stock

4 Ounces salt Make paste of flour and soup stock. Boil 3 minutes and add salt

Pour over vegetables and fill cans. NUMBER OF
MINUTES TO STERILIZE

In boiling water or homemade outfit, 212
degrees Fahrenheit, 90.
In condensed steam outfit, 90.
In water-seal outfit, 214 degrees Fahrenheit,
75.
In steam-pressure outfit, 5 pounds, 75.
In pressure-cooker outfit, 10 to 15 pounds,
45.

CREAM OF PEA SOUP

INGREDIENTS NUMBER OF
MINUTES
TO BLANCH OTHER PREPARATION 8 Pounds
dried peas Soak over-night and cook until soft.
Mash peas fine. 5 Gallons soup stock Add stock
and boil. Put through sieve. ½ Pound flour
10 Ounces sugar
3 Ounces salt Make paste of flour, sugar and salt
and add to stock. Cook until thick.
Can. NUMBER OF MINUTES TO STERILIZE

In boiling water or homemade outfit, 212
degrees Fahrenheit, 90.
In condensed steam outfit, 90.
In water-seal outfit, 214 degrees Fahrenheit,
80.
In steam-pressure outfit, 5 pounds, 70.

In pressure-cooker outfit, 10 to 15 pounds, 45.

CREAM OF POTATO SOUP

INGREDIENTS NUMBER OF
MINUTES
TO BLANCH OTHER PREPARATION 1½
Pounds potatoes sliced thin
5 Gallons soup stock
3 Ounces salt
¼ Teaspoonful pepper
½ Pound butter
3 Tablespoonfuls flour Boil potatoes and stock
10 minutes.
Add salt, pepper, butter and boil
5 minutes. Make flour
into paste and add.
Cook 3 minutes and can. NUMBER OF MINUTES
TO STERILIZE

In boiling water or homemade outfit, 212 degrees Fahrenheit, 90.

In condensed steam outfit, 90.

In water-seal outfit, 214 degrees Fahrenheit, 75.

In steam-pressure outfit, 5 pounds, 65.

In pressure-cooker outfit, 10 to 15 pounds, 45.

BEAN SOUP

INGREDIENTS NUMBER OF
MINUTES
TO BLANCH OTHER PREPARATION 3 Pounds
dried beans Soak 12 hours. 2 Pounds ham Cut ham
into ¼ inch cubes. 4 Gallons water
5 Gallons soup stock
Salt Boil beans, ham and water
until beans are soft.
Mash beans fine. Add
stock and salt. Can. NUMBER OF MINUTES TO
STERILIZE

In boiling water or homemade outfit, 212
degrees Fahrenheit, 120.
In condensed steam outfit, 120.
In water-seal outfit, 214 degrees Fahrenheit,
90.
In steam-pressure outfit, 5 pounds, 75.
In pressure-cooker outfit, 10 to 15 pounds,
60.

CHICKEN SOUP STOCK (Foundation of All
Chicken Soups)

INGREDIENTS NUMBER OF
MINUTES
TO BLANCH OTHER PREPARATION 30
Pounds chicken
10 Gallons cold water.
Should make 10 gallons
stock when finished Simmer 5 hours. Can.
NUMBER OF MINUTES TO STERILIZE

In boiling water or homemade outfit, 212 degrees Fahrenheit, 90.

In condensed steam outfit, 90.

In water-seal outfit, 214 degrees Fahrenheit, 75.

In steam-pressure outfit, 5 pounds, 60.

In pressure-cooker outfit, 10 to 15 pounds, 45.

CHICKEN GUMBO

INGREDIENTS NUMBER OF
MINUTES
TO BLANCH OTHER PREPARATION 2 Pounds ham Cut ham into small cubes and boil 30 minutes. 3 Pounds chicken Mince chicken. ½ Pound onions Chop onions. ½ Pound flour Make paste of flour. 5 Gallons chicken soup stock
½ Pound butter
¼ Pound salt
3 Ounces powdered okra
mixed with pint of
water Add all this to soup stock.
Add butter and salt. Boil
10 minutes. Then add
okra mixed with water.
Can. NUMBER OF MINUTES TO STERILIZE

In boiling water or homemade outfit, 212 degrees Fahrenheit, 90.

In condensed steam outfit, 90.
In water-seal outfit, 214 degrees Fahrenheit,
75.
In steam-pressure outfit, 5 pounds, 60.
In pressure-cooker outfit, 10 to 15 pounds,
45.

CHAPTER VI

JELLIES, JAMS, PRESERVES, MARMALADES,
FRUIT JUICES AND SIRUPS

For jelly making select firm, slightly
underripe fruit that is fairly acid and contains a
large amount of pectin. Fruit that is just a little
underripe contains more pectin than the mature or
overripe fruits. Pectin is the substance that makes
jelly harden. This fundamental jelly-making quality
does not exist in all fruits. Such fruits as currants,
crab apples and grapes contain much pectin and are,
therefore, considered excellent jelly-making fruits.

The white inner skin of grapefruit is also a
prolific source of pectin, but as it has a bitter taste
we seldom use it for jellies, though we find it
valuable in making orange, grapefruit and other
marmalades.

Rhubarb, strawberries and cherries all lack
pectin, but can be made into good jellies if we add
the white skins of oranges and lemons to them
while cooking.

So the very first thing we must know about jelly making is whether or not a fruit contains pectin. There will be no tears shed over jelly that will not "jell" if all young housewives will learn the simple test for pectin; to find out whether a juice contains pectin or not is a very easy matter.

Take one tablespoonful of grain alcohol—90 to 95 per cent.—and add to it one tablespoonful of *cooked* juice that has been cooled. The effect of the alcohol is to bring together the pectin in a jelly-like mass. If a large quantity of pectin is present it will appear in one mass or clot which may be gathered up on a spoon. You will notice I said *cooked* juice. It is peculiar that this pectin frequently is not found in the juices of raw fruits, though it is very plentiful in the cooked juices. Therefore the test must be made with cooked juice.

There is little pectin in the juice of raw apples, raw quince, raw grapes, and yet the cooked juices are full of pectin.

This test not only indicates the amount of pectin present, but it also gives some idea of the proper proportions of sugar to juice. If three-fourths or more of the juice forms a gelatinous mass or clot this indicates that you should use three-fourths as much sugar as juice. If the pectin is slightly gelatinous or is less than three-fourths of the whole volume of juice, use less sugar. If the pectin is less than one-half add some form of pectin to make the jelly, or can the juice for use as a beverage, for flavoring ice cream or some form of cooking.

By employing this test, sugar can often be reduced, and thus the jelly texture will be fine, less rubbery and the flavor will be better.

After the fruit has been selected and

prepared as usual by washing, stemming, and so forth, it is ready to be heated in an acid-proof kettle. With juicy fruits use just enough water to prevent burning—about one cup of water to every four or five quarts of fruit. The juicy fruits are currants, raspberries, and so forth. With less juicy fruits, as apples or quinces, use enough water to cover, or follow the rule, half as much water as fruit. Use the cores, skins and seeds; these improve the flavor and color of the jelly.

Berries can be mashed. Heat the fruit slowly in a covered kettle, stirring once in a while to obtain an even cooking. When the simmering point is reached, crush the fruit with a well-soaked wooden masher. When the fruit is tender or has a transparent appearance, it is ready to strain.

The jelly bag must be of closely woven material; one with a large mouth is advisable. If cheesecloth is used double it and tie opposite corners together. When a very clear jelly is desired use a flannel or felt bag for straining the juice.

What drips into the dish or pan is called Extraction One. When this Extraction One is fairly drained out, which takes about thirty minutes, do not squeeze the pulp for a second grade jelly as so many housewives do; instead, make another juice extraction. To do this, empty the contents or pulp in the bag into the preserving kettle, cover with water, and stir until thoroughly mixed; then cover, bring slowly to a boil as before and drain again. The juice that drips out is called Extraction Two.

The pectin-alcohol test can be used here again to find out whether there is much or little or no pectin left. If much pectin is present, you can repeat the operation and get Extraction Three.

Three extractions usually exhaust the pectin, but sometimes you can get as many as five extractions.

You may say, "Why bother with extractions—why not squeeze the juice and be done with it?" You will get clearer, better-flavored and more glasses of jelly if you will make the extractions than if you squeeze the jelly bag.

I always make the jelly from Extraction One by itself, but usually combine Extraction Two and Three.

The next step in jelly making is vitally important—that is, how much sugar to use to a given amount of fruit juice. This is where many housewives "fall down" on jelly making. They use the same proportion of sugar to all juices.

To make jelly that does not crystallize the right proportion of sugar must be added to the juice. To make jelly that is not tough or unpleasantly sour, the right proportion of sugar and juice must be used.

Currants and unripe or partly ripened grapes are so rich in pectin that they require equal amounts of sugar and juice—that is, to every cup of extracted currant and grape juice we add one cup of sugar.

Red raspberries and blackberries require three-fourths of a cup of sugar to every cup of juice. All fruits which require much water in the cooking take three-fourths of a cup of sugar to every cup of juice. Crab apples and cranberries are examples.

It is harder to make jellies from the fruits to which a large amount of water is added than from the juicy fruits.

I am frequently asked, "When should you add the sugar to the fruit juice in jelly making? Do you add it at the beginning of the boiling, in the middle of the process, or at the end, and should the sugar be hot when added to the juice?" It is better to add the sugar in the middle of the jelly-making process than at the beginning or the end. Skim the juice well before adding the sugar, so as to lose as little sugar as possible.

If the sugar is hot when added it will not cool the juice, and thus the cooking time will be shortened. To heat the sugar put it in a granite dish, place in the oven, leaving the oven door ajar, and stir occasionally. Be careful not to scorch it.

After the juice is put on, the jelly making should be done as quickly as possible. No simmering should be allowed and no violent boiling. A steady boiling, for as few minutes as possible, will produce good results.

Currant, blueberry and grape jelly usually can be made in from eight to ten minutes. The hot sugar is added at the end of four or five minutes.

Raspberry, blackberry and apple jelly take from twenty to thirty minutes. The sugar is added at the end of ten or fifteen minutes.

The jellying point is hard to determine. If you have a cooking thermometer or candy thermometer always use it when making jelly. It is the one sure, reliable test.

The temperature for jellies is 221 degrees Fahrenheit. If you want a very soft jelly, boil it 220 degrees. If you want to use it immediately, then boil it to 222 degrees.

If you do not have a thermometer the next best test is to pour the boiling sirup from the side of a clean, hot spoon, held horizontally. If the sirup is done two drops will break simultaneously from the side of the spoon.

Another test is to take a little jelly on a cold plate and draw a path through it with the point of a spoon; if the path stays and the juice does not run together, the jellying point has been reached.

When the jellying point has been reached, remove the kettle from the fire, skim the jelly and pour immediately into hot, sterilized glasses, which have been set on a cloth wrung out of hot water to prevent breaking. Fill the glasses not quite full.

Never attempt to make more than six to eight glasses of jelly at one time. If new at the game make only four, because there is danger of the juice jellying in the kettle before it can be removed.

When the jellies are well set cover them with *hot*, not merely melted, paraffin. The paraffin if hot will kill any germs that may fall on the surface of the jelly. Then cover with the clean tin or aluminum covers and store the jelly in a dry, cool place after proper labeling.

STEPS IN JELLY MAKING

1. Select firm, slightly underripe fruit that is fairly acid and contains a large amount of pectin.

2. Prepare fruit as usual by washing, stemming, and so forth.

3. Heat slowly in acid-proof kettle until fruit is tender. Mash berries before beginning to cook them. A little water may be added if necessary to keep from burning. Cut hard fruits into small pieces; add half as much water as fruit.

4. Pour into dampened bag.

5. Drain through closely woven bag.

6. Make alcohol test for pectin to determine

minimum amount of sugar to use, also the character of the fruit. The amount of pectin, the fundamental jelly-making property, varies in different fruits. To make the pectin test add to one tablespoonful of cold cooked fruit juice one tablespoonful of grain alcohol. Shake gently. Allow to stand one-half hour. If three-fourths or more of the juice forms a lump add three-fourths as much sugar as juice in making jelly. If the precipitate—pectin—is not held together in a lump or is less than three-fourths of the whole volume of juice, add less sugar in proportion to juice. If less than one-half forms a lump, add pectin to make the jelly, or can the juice for use as a beverage, flavoring, and so forth.

7. If fruit juice meets jelly-making test put on to cook.

8. Add required amount of sugar after juice begins to boil or midway in the process.

9. Stir until sugar is dissolved.

10. Cook rapidly, but not hard.

11. Test to determine when jelly stage is reached by dipping a clean spoon into boiling juice. Remove and allow juice to drip from it. If done, two drops will break simultaneously from side of spoon. Some prefer to wait until mass sheets off from side of spoon. Better still, use thermometer.

12. Remove from fire and skim.

13. Pour immediately into hot, sterilized glasses.

14. When cool add hot melted paraffin. Melt the paraffin in a little coffeepot or pitcher with spout, so it will pour easily.

15. Cover, label and store.

No time can be given for jelly making, for several things enter into consideration: The proportion of pectin in the juice, the amount of water used in cooking the fruit and the proportion of sugar to juice; the more sugar used, the less time needed.

JAMS AND BUTTERS

Jams and butters are not so difficult to make as jellies.

1. Carefully wash berries and fruits.

2. Weigh the fruit on standard scales or, if scales are not convenient, use measuring cup.

3. Mash berries. Cut large fruits into several pieces.

4. Add enough water to prevent sticking.

5. Stir to keep from burning.

6. Cook gently until the mass begins to thicken.

7. Measure sugar, using three-fourths part of sugar to one part fruit. That is, for every pound of fruit use three-fourths of a pound of sugar, or to every cup of fruit use three-fourths of a cup of sugar.

8. Continue cooking, allowing the jam to simmer gently.

9. Cook the mixture until the desired consistency is reached. When a little of the jam falls in heavy drops from the spoon, it is thick enough.

10. A small amount of mixed ground spices, vinegar or crystallized ginger can be added if desired.

11. Pour into hot, sterilized glasses to within one-half inch of the top.

12. Allow to cool, seal with paraffin, cover,

label and store.

Fruit butters are always softer than jam. Marmalades are made much as are jams. The rind is usually used in lemon, orange and grapefruit marmalades.

Conserves consist of a combination of several fruits. Nuts and raisins are often added to conserves.

Preserves are thick mixtures containing sugar equal to at least three-fourths of the weight of the fruit.

If you wish to eliminate the necessity of using paraffin or other wax tops for jellies, jams and preserves, you can use the cold-pack method of canning. You may have containers with screw or bail tops which you wish to use in this way. The following is one recipe showing how to proceed.

Cherry Preserves. Place one gallon of water in a kettle and add ten pounds of pitted cherries. Boil slowly for eighteen minutes. Add twelve pounds of granulated sugar and cook until product is boiling at a temperature of 219 degrees. Cool quickly in shallow pans. Pack into glass jars. Put rubber and cap in position, not tight. Cap and tip if using enameled tin cans. If using a hot-water-bath outfit, sterilize twenty minutes; if using a water-seal outfit, a five-pound steam-pressure outfit or a pressure-cooker outfit, sterilize fifteen minutes. Remove jars. Tighten covers. Invert to cool and test the joints. Wrap jars with paper to prevent bleaching and store. When using pressure-cooker outfits on preserves, keep the valve open during period of sterilization.

Fruit Juices. Fruit juices furnish a healthful and delicious drink and are readily canned at home.

Grapes, raspberries and other small fruits may be crushed in a fruit press or put in a cloth sack, heated for thirty minutes, or until the juice runs freely, and allowed to drip.

Strain through two thicknesses of cotton flannel to remove the sediment, sweeten slightly, bottle, close by filling the neck of the bottle with a thick pad of sterilized cotton, heat to 160 degrees, or until air bubbles begin to form on the bottom of the cooker, and keep at this temperature one hour and a half to two hours; or heat to 200 degrees, or until the bubbles begin to rise to the top of the water, and hold at this temperature for thirty minutes. The hot water comes up to the neck of the bottle. Cork without removing the cotton. If canned in jars close the jar partly, and seal tight after cooking.

Fruit juices should never be heated above 200 degrees, as a higher temperature injures the flavor.

Strawberry Preserves. 1. Add thirty-five ounces of sugar to one-half pint of water; bring to a boil and skim.

With this amount of sirup the berries can be packed attractively without floating and no sirup will be left over.

To this amount of sirup add exactly two and three-fourths pounds of washed, capped and stemmed strawberries. Boil the fruit until it registers 222 degrees Fahrenheit on a candy or chemical thermometer. If no thermometer is available boil until the sirup is very heavy—about as thick as molasses. Remove the scum.

Fill the sterilized jars full of hot berries. Pour in enough of the hot sirup to fill the jar, leaving as little air space as possible. Put sterilized rings and caps on at once, but do not fasten tightly.

Stand the sealed jars in tepid water up to their necks if possible. Bring this water to a boil. Let pint jars stay in the boiling water for at least fifteen minutes and quart jars at least twenty-five minutes; then close caps tightly at once. At the conclusion of the operation, stand each jar for a moment on its cap to make sure that the seal is absolutely tight.

Recipe Number 2. The following method is preferred by some because it leaves more of the natural color in the preserves:

To two pounds of washed, capped and stemmed strawberries add twenty-six ounces sugar; let stand over-night. In the morning pour juice thus obtained into a preserving kettle, add berries and cook to 222 degrees Fahrenheit, or until the sirup is very heavy. Pack and sterilize, as in Recipe Number 1. These recipes can be used for all other berries.

When wet weather makes strawberries too soft or sandy for the table, they are still useful for making "strawberry acid," a thick sirup which, mixed with water, ice and perhaps spearmint, makes a cooling summer drink.

Strawberries—Sun Preserves. Select firm ripe berries; hull and rinse. Place them in a shallow platter in a single layer; sprinkle sugar over them. Pour over them a thick sirup made of one quart of water and eleven pounds of sugar, boiled until very thick.

Cover them with a glass dish or a plain window glass. Allow them to stand in the hot sun eight to twelve hours. Pack them in jelly glasses and cover with paraffin or put in regular glass jars or tin cans. Put the rubber and cap in position, not tight. Cap and tip or seal if using enameled tin cans. Sterilize for the length of time given below for the particular type of outfit used:

MINUTES Hot-water bath, homemade or commercial 20 Water seal, 214 degrees 15 Steam pressure 10   Remove the jars, tighten the covers, invert the jars to cool, and test the joint. Wrap the jars in paper to prevent bleaching.

When using steam-pressure or pressure-cooking outfit on preserves, remember to keep the valve open during the sterilizing.

SPECIAL DIRECTIONS FOR JELLY AND JAM MAKING

Apples vary in the percentage of sugar and acid they contain; a fine flavored acid apple should be used when possible. Winter apples are best for jelly making. If necessary to make apple jelly in the spring, add juice of 1 lemon to every pint of apple juice.

Apricots are delicious combined with pineapple.

Blackberries, elderberries and loganberries make delicious juices and shrubs for summer beverages.

The total time of making blueberry jelly need not exceed 10 minutes.

Cranberries are not always put through a jelly bag, but are rubbed through a sieve.

Cherries are most delicious if preserved in the sun. A good combination for preserves is equal parts of cherries and strawberries.

Crab apples can be combined with some juices, such as peach, pear and pineapple, to furnish necessary pectin.

One-half currants and one-half raspberries make a delicious jelly; currants are in best condition for jelly making from June 28 to July 3.

Black currant jam is considered quite a delicacy these days.

Acid grapes are best for jelly; sweet, ripe grapes contain too much sugar. Equal portions ripe and green grapes are satisfactory.

If gooseberries are fully ripe they make finer-flavored jam than do green-as-grass gooseberries.

Some women are successful in making peach jelly, but be sure to test for pectin before completing the process, to save time and effort.

Pineapple is best canned alone or used as foundation for conserves.

An underripe, acid plum is best.

Plums and apples combined make an excellent tasting jelly.

Quince parings are often used for jelly, the better part of the fruit being used for preserving.

Raspberries and other berries should not be gathered after a rain, for they will have absorbed so much water as to make it difficult, without excessive boiling, to get the juice to "jell."

Rhubarb is an excellent foundation for the more expensive fruit. It will take the flavor of other fruits and thus we can make an otherwise expensive jam "go a long way."

Strawberries combine well with other fruits and can be utilized in many ways.

Select sour, smooth-skinned oranges.

Lemon Marmalade. After the 9 oranges and 6 lemons are sliced, put in kettle; add 4 quarts water, cover and let stand 36 hours; then boil 2 hours. Add 8 pounds sugar and boil one hour longer.

Grapefruit used alone is bitter. Oranges or lemons or both are usually combined with grapefruit.

All wild fruits or berries used for jelly making must be fresh and not overripe. Barberry jelly is firmer and of better color if made from fruit picked before the frost comes, while some of the berries are still green.

CHART FOR JELLY AND JAM MAKING KIND OF FRUIT CHARACTER OF FRUIT HOW TO PREPARE AMOUNT OF WATER NEEDED FOR COOKING AMOUNT OF SUGAR NEEDED FOR JELLYING APPLES, SOUR Excellent for jelly making Wash, discard any unsound portions, cut into small pieces. Include seeds skin and core One-half as much water as fruit ¾ cupful of sugar to 1 cupful of juice APRICOTS Not suitable for jelly making. Excellent for jam. Leave a few stones in for flavor. For jam use just enough water to keep from burning ¾ cupful of sugar to 1 cupful of apricots for jam BLACKBERRIES Excellent for jelly making Wash 1 cupful of water to 5 quarts of berries ¾ cupful of sugar to 1 cupful of juice BLUEBERRIES Excellent for jelly making; make a sweet jelly Wash 1 cupful of water to 5 quarts of berries 1 cupful of sugar to 1 cupful of juice CRANBERRIES Excellent for jelly making Wash One-half as much water as berries ¾ cupful of sugar to 1 cupful of juice CHERRIES Pectin must be added for jelly making Pit the cherries for jam For jam, use just enough water to keep from burning ¾ cupful of sugar to 1 cupful of cherries for jam CRAB APPLES Excellent for jelly making Same as apples One-half as much water as apples ¾ cupful of sugar to 1 cupful of juice CURRANTS, RED Excellent for jelly making Do not remove stems for jelly 1 cupful of water to 5 quarts of currants 1 cupful of sugar to 1 cupful of juice CURRANTS, BLACK Better for jam Remove stems Enough water to keep from sticking ¾ cupful of sugar to 1 cupful of currants GRAPES, UNRIPE Excellent for jelly making Wash, do not stem; use stems 1 cupful of water to 5 quarts of grapes 1 cupful of sugar to 1 cupful of juice GOOSEBERRIES Excellent for jelly making "Head and tail," using scissors 1 cupful of water to 5 quarts of gooseberries 1 cupful of sugar to 1 cupful of juice PEACHES Pectin must be added for jelly making Peaches, apples and raisins make a delicious conserve Just enough water to keep from burning ¾ cupful of sugar to 1 cupful of juice PINEAPPLES Pectin must be added for jelly making Prepare as for table use For jams, enough water to keep from burning ¾ cupful of sugar to 1 cupful of juice PLUMS, GREENGAGE Suitable for jelly making Mash fruit and remove stems; cook stones with fruit 1 quart of water for each peck of fruit ¾ cupful of sugar to 1 cupful of juice PLUMS, DAMSON Suitable for jelly making Wipe and pick over; prick several times with large pin 1 quart of water for every peck of plums ¾ cupful of sugar to 1 cupful of juice QUINCES Excellent for jelly making, if not too ripe. If so, add crab apple Cut out the blossom end. Mash and cut in quarters One-half as much water as quinces ¾ cupful of sugar to 1 cupful of juice RASPBERRIES Excellent for jelly making Wash them thoroughly, but do not let them soak in the water 1 cupful of water to 5 quarts of berries 1 cupful of sugar to 1 cupful of juice RHUBARB Pectin must be added for jelly making. Better for jam. Wash and cut into small pieces For jam, half as much water as fruit. ¾ cupful of sugar to 1 cupful of juice STRAWBERRIES Pectin must be added for jelly making. Wash and remove hulls. For jam, just enough water to keep from burning. ¾ cupful of sugar to 1 cupful of pulp. CITRUS FRUITS ORANGES Excellent for jelly making and marmalade For orange marmalade weigh oranges slice cross- wise with sharp knife as thin as possible; remove seed. Cook in water to cover. Three-quarters their weight in sugar. LEMONS Excellent for jelly making and to supply pectin to other fruits For marmalade 9 oranges and 6 lemons are a good combination   8 pounds of sugar GRAPEFRUIT Best for marmalades Grapefruit is sliced very thin, seed removed.   Three-quarters their weight in sugar. WILD FRUITS RASPBERRIES, BLACKBERRIES, BARBERRIES, GRAPES, BEACH PLUMS. All excellent for jelly making. Prepare as other fruits. Just enough water to keep from burning. 1 cupful of sugar to 1 cupful of juice.

CHAPTER VII

MEAT

Canned meat adds variety to the diet in the winter-time and makes a pleasant change from the cured and smoked meats. You put meat into jars in the raw state and extend the sterilizing period or you can cook the meat partially or completely and then sterilize for a shorter period of time. Of course a reliable method of canning meat must be used, such as the cold-pack process, where the sterilizing is done in the tin or jar in either boiling water or steam under pressure. We usually recommend the partial cooking, roasting or boiling of the meat before canning especially for beginners. If you are a beginner in the business of cold-pack canning then by all means cook the meat before putting it in cans. If you have canned peas, beans and corn successfully for years then you are ready for all kinds of raw meat canning.

To save criticism of the cold-pack method of canning meat and to guard against any danger from eating poorly prepared and improperly sterilized meat we do not urge beginners to experiment with meat, although the meat can be safely canned by any one whether new at the canning game or a veteran in it if directions are carefully followed. But it is the big "If" that we have to watch.

Many farmers and farmerettes are canning meats of all kinds all over the country and there is never a can lost. We need more meat canning done at home and you can do it if you will practice cleanliness in all your work and follow directions.

The fear of getting botulinus bacteria from eating canned meat is just a "bug-a-boo." It should be clearly understood that botulism is one of the very rare maladies. The chances for getting it by eating canned goods, say the experts, is rather less than the chances from dying of lockjaw every time you scratch your finger. To regard every can as a source of botulism is worse than regarding every dog as a source of hydrophobia. Moreover, for the very timid, there is the comforting certainty that the exceedingly slight danger is completely eliminated by re-cooking the canned food for a short time before eating it.

There are always a few cases of illness traceable to bad food, not only to canned food but to spoiled meats, fish, bad milk, oysters and a number of things. There are also cases of injury and death by street accidents, but we do not for that reason stop using the streets. If you put good meat into the can and do your canning right then you will have good results. Never put into a can meat that is about ready to spoil, thinking thereby to "save it."

If you want to be absolutely sure, even if the jar of meat seems perfectly fresh when it is opened, you can re-cook the meat, thus insuring yourself against any possibility of botulinus poisoning. So you see, there is nothing at all alarming about that frightful sounding word "botulinus." Using fresh products, doing the canning properly and reheating before serving eliminates all danger.

For canning meat, tin cans are in most respects superior to glass, as they eliminate all danger of breakage, preserve the meat just as well as glass, and by excluding the light prevent any change of color. If you use glass jars be sure to get the best brand of jar rubbers on the market. This is very important.

If, as I have said, you are a beginner—cook the meat first by frying, roasting, broiling, baking or stewing—just as you would prepare it for immediate use. The meat is usually seasoned according to taste and is cooked until thoroughly heated through, before putting in the cans. Do not cook until tender as that will be too long with the additional sterilizing. If too tender it will fall apart and be unappetizing although perfectly good. See that nothing is wasted in the canning. If you are canning a young steer or a calf you would go about it as follows:

Select the meat that you would ordinarily want. Slice the meat wanted for steak. What is not suited for either of these can be used for stews, or be put through the meat grinder and made into sausage meat, formed into little cakes, fried and canned. What meat is left clinging to all bones will be utilized when the bones are boiled for soup stock. The sinews, the head and the feet, after being cleaned may be used for soup stock also.

The liver should be soaked in water, the coarse veins cut out and the liver skinned and prepared any way that is desired before canning it or it may be made into liver sausage. The heart can be used for goulash. The kidneys should be soaked in salt water, split open and the little sack removed; then they can be either stewed or fried and then canned. The sweetbreads may be prepared in various ways and then canned.

The brain is soaked in water to remove the blood, and the membrane enclosing it is removed. It

can be fried or prepared in any favorite way and
then canned. The ox tail is used for soup. The
tongue is soaked in water, scrubbed, cleaned, salted,
boiled, skinned and packed in cans with some soup
stock added.

If you do not care to use the head for soup
stock and if it comes from a young animal, split it
open and soak in cold water. Use a brush and scrub
thoroughly. Remove the eyes and mucous
membrane of the nostrils and then boil it. After it is
boiled, remove all meat and make a mock turtle
stew or ragout. Prepare the tripe as for table use and
then can.

After the soup stock is made and the bones
are cracked for a second cooking, the bones need
not be thrown away. You can dry them, run them
through a bone crusher and either feed them to the
chickens or use them for fertilizer. In this way not a
particle of the dressed animal is wasted.

Here are a few ways to utilize the cuts that
are really "left-overs."

GOULASH
2 Pounds of meat scraps which can consist
of beef, veal or pork.
2 Ounces of any fat.
2 Onions chopped fine.
1 Stalk celery, cut in small pieces.
2 Carrots.
2 Cups tomatoes either canned or fresh.
1 Bay leaf.
6 Whole cloves.
6 Peppercorns.
1 Blade mace or a little thyme or both.

A little flour.

1 Tablespoonful chopped parsley.

Salt and paprika to taste.

Cut the meat into one inch squares and roll in flour. Melt the fat in the frying pan, add the vegetables (onions, celery, carrots) and brown lightly: add the meat and brown. Stir with a spoon or fork to prevent burning. When browned empty into a pan.

Put the bay leaf, cloves, peppercorns, mace and thyme into a cheesecloth bag and add to the meat, add tomatoes. Cover with soup stock or water and simmer 45 minutes if it is going to be canned. If for immediate use, 2 hours will be necessary to thoroughly cook it.

Remove the spices, season with salt, paprika and the chopped parsley. You can add Worcestershire sauce or soy sauce if desired. Use only small quantities as these sauces are very strong in their distinctive flavor. Put hot mixture into cans and sterilize.

If the different spices are not at hand a good goulash can be made by using the meat, fat, onions, tomatoes, flour, salt and pepper and omitting the rest of the recipe.

LIVER SAUSAGE

Beef, veal, or hog liver. Remove the membrane and cut away the large blood vessels. Soak in water 1 to 2 hours to draw out blood. Boil until done. When cooled put through a food chopper or grate finely. Take half as much boiled fat pork as liver. Divide this fat into two portions; chop one portion into one-quarter inch cubes; pass the other portion through the food chopper; mix all together thoroughly; add salt, ground cloves, pepper, and a little grated onion to taste. A little thyme and marjoram may be added to suit taste. (For a liver weighing 1½ pounds add ¾ pounds fat pork, 3 to 4 teaspoonfuls salt, ½ teaspoonful cloves, ½ teaspoonful pepper, 1 small onion, ¼ teaspoonful thyme, and pinch of marjoram.) This mixture is stuffed into large casings. (If no casings are available, make casings of clean white muslin.) Cover with boiling water, bring to a boil, and boil for 10 minutes. Pack into cans, fill in with the water in which the sausages were boiled. Sterilize.

This liver sausage may also be made from the raw liver and raw pork, but in that case the sterilizing is for a longer period, as the time-table indicates. This recipe is recommended by the United States Department of Agriculture.

HEAD CHEESE

Cut a hog's head into four pieces. Remove the brains, ears, skin, snout and eyes. Cut off the fattest parts for lard. Put the lean and bony parts to soak over night in cold water in order to extract the blood and dirt. When the head is cleaned put it over the fire to boil, using water enough to cover it. Boil until the meat separates readily from the bones. Then remove it from the fire and pick out all the bones. Drain off the liquor, saving a part of it for future use. Chop the meat up finely with a chopping knife. Return it to the kettle and pour on enough of the liquor to cover the meat. Let it boil slowly for fifteen minutes to a half-hour. Season to taste with salt and pepper just before removing it from the fire. Bay leaves, a little ground cloves and allspice may be added and boiled a short time in the soup. Pack while hot in cans to within ½ inch of top. Sterilize. This head cheese is always served cold.

CORNED BEEF

After beef has been properly corned for three weeks, remove the meat from the brine. Soak for two hours in clear water, changing water once. Place in a wire basket and boil slowly for half an hour. Remove from the boiling water, plunge into cold water, and remove gristle, bone and excessive fat. Cut into small pieces and pack closely into cans. Add no salt and proceed as in other canning.

CANNED PORK

After the animal has been killed, cool quickly and keep the pork cool for at least 24 hours. Can only lean portions, using the fat to make lard. Place meat in a wire basket or cheesecloth and boil 30 minutes, or roast in the oven for 30 minutes. Cut into small sections and pack closely into cans. Add salt and proceed with remainder of process.

Other pieces of beef and pork: Hamburg steak, sausage, venison, squirrel, raccoon, opossum, lamb, are canned as follows:

After cleaning, season and fry, roast, stew, or bake in oven as though preparing for serving directly on the table. Cook until meat is about three fourths done. Pack while hot into sanitary tin cans or glass jars. Pour over the meat the hot liquids, gravies, dressings, etc., or hot water. Add salt and proceed as in any other cold-pack canning.

HOW TO CAN POULTRY AND GAME WITH THE BONES REMOVED

Kill bird and draw immediately; wash carefully and cool; then cut into convenient sections. Boil until the meat can be removed from the bones; remove from the boiling liquid and take out all bones; pack closely into glass jars or enameled cans; fill jars with the hot liquid after it has been concentrated one half; add 1 level teaspoonful salt to every quart of meat for seasoning; put rubbers and top of jars in place but not tight. If using enameled cans completely seal. Sterilize the length of time given in the time-table on page 108 of this book. After the sterilizing remove the jars; tighten the covers if glass was used; invert to cool and test joints. Wrap with paper to prevent bleaching.

FRIED SPRING CHICKEN

After cleaning and preparing the chickens, season and fry as though for serving directly on the table. Cook until the meat is about three-fourths done. If a whole spring chicken, break the neck and both legs and fold around body of chicken. Roll up tight, tie a string around the chicken and drop this hot, partially fried product into sanitary tin cans or glass jars. A quart tin can (No. 3) will hold two to four small chickens. Pour liquid from the griddle or frying pan into the can over the chicken. Proceed, as in any other canning, with the sealing, sterilizing and removing of the jars. Chicken fries canned in the late fall preserve the meat at the most delicious stage and furthermore we avoid the expense of feeding the chickens throughout the winter.

HOW TO CAN COCKERELS

When cockerels reach the point in their growth where it is no longer profitable to feed them, and when they are wanted for home use during the winter months they should be canned. This method of handling the cockerel not only saves money by cutting down the feed bill, but it places in the pantry or cellar the means of a delicious chicken dinner at a time of the year when the price of poultry is high.

The bird should not be fed for at least twenty-four hours before killing. It should be killed by the approved method and picked dry. When the feathers have been removed and the pin feathers drawn the bird should be cooled rapidly. This rapid cooling after killing is essential to a good flavor in canned meat. As soon as the bird has been properly cooled it should be singed and washed carefully with a brush.

CUTTING UP AND DRAWING CHICKENS

Mr. George Farrell, a most expert canner,

tells us how to go about this job of canning chicken.

In preparing the bird for canning, care should be taken in drawing it so that the contents of the digestive tract do not come in contact with the meat.

1. Remove the tops of the wings, cutting at the first joint.

2. Remove the wings.

3. Remove the foot, cutting at the knee joint.

4. Remove the leg, cutting at the hip or saddle joint.

5. Cut the removed portion of the leg into two parts at the joint.

6. Place the bird so the back of the head is toward the operator, cut through the neck bone with a sharp knife but do not cut the windpipe or gullet.

7. With the index finger separate the gullet and windpipe from the skin of the neck.

8. Cut through the skin of the neck.

9. With a pointed knife cut through the skin from the upper part of the neck, thus separated, to the wing.

10. Leave the head attached to the gullet and windpipe and loosen these from the neck down as far as the crop.

11. With a sharp pointed knife cut around the shoulder blade, pull it out of position and break it.

12. Find the white spots on the ribs and cut through the ribs on these white spots.

13. Cut back to the vent; cut around it, and loosen.

14. Begin at the crop and remove the digestive tract from the bird, pulling it back toward the vent.

15. Remove the lungs and kidneys with the point of a knife.

16. Cut off the neck close to the body.

17. Cut through the backbone at the joint or just above the diaphragm.

18. Remove the oil sack.

19. Separate the breast from the backbone by cutting through on the white spots.

20. Cut the fillet from each side of the breastbone.

21. Cut in sharp at the point of the breastbone, turning the knife and cutting away the wishbone with the meat. Bend in the bones of the breastbone.

PACKING CHICKEN

Use a one quart jar. Caution: Do not pack the giblets with the meat.

1. Have the jar hot.

2. Pack the saddle with a thigh inside.

3. Pack the breastbone with a thigh inside.

4. Pack the backbone and ribs with a leg inside.

5. Pack the legs large end downward, alongside the breastbone.

6. Pack the wings.

7. Pack the wishbone.

8. Pack the fillets.

9. Pack the neck-bone.

10. Pour on boiling water to within one inch of the top; add a level teaspoonful of salt; place the rubber and cap in position, partially seal, and sterilize for the length of time given below for the

particular type of outfit used:

Water bath, home made or commercial (pint or quart jars) 1 hour

Water seal, 214° 3 hours

5 pounds steam-pressure 2 hours

10 to 15 pounds steam-pressure 1 hour

Remove jars; tighten covers; invert to cool, and test joints. Wrap jars with paper to prevent bleaching.

PIGEONS

Young pigeons. Dress pigeons, wash well, and roast for 30 minutes basting frequently. Some pieces of fat bacon put over the breasts will prevent them getting too dry.

Old pigeons. Dress, wash, and fry pigeons.

Brown some onions in the fat with the pigeons, using a pound of onions to a dozen birds. Cover with hot water after pigeons and onions are a golden brown; simmer until the meat is tender and can be removed from the bones. Add from time to time boiling water, if necessary, in order to keep the birds covered. When tender, take meat from bones. Return the meat to the liquor, salt to taste and pack while boiling into cans or jars, fill with liquor to within one-half inch of top.

All small game birds may be canned like pigeons. Blackbirds may be treated like pigeons. They make an excellent stew.

PLAIN CANNING OF TENDER COTTON-TAILS OR TWICE-SKINNED JACK-RABBITS

1. Blanch in boiling water until the meat is white.

2. Cold dip.

3. Pack tightly in sterilized jars.

4. Add boiling water and 1 teaspoonful salt to quart.

5. Adjust rubber and lid.

6. Sterilize in hot water bath for three hours.

7. Remove from bath and complete the seal.

Rabbit meat thus canned, may be served in various appetizing ways.

RABBIT SAUSAGE

For rabbit sausage and mince-meat only the backs and legs of the carcass are used, discarding the sinews.

Grind together equal parts of rabbit and fat pork (or at least ¼ fat pork). The pork may be salt pork if all salt is omitted from the mixture.

To every ten pounds of the above add 6 teaspoonfuls salt, 1 teaspoonful of pepper, 2 teaspoonfuls powdered sage. Mix thoroughly. Shape in flat cakes and fry till nicely browned. Pack tightly in jars, pour over the fat in which the sausage was fried, and sterilize.

RABBIT MINCE-MEAT

Rabbit mince-meat is used a great deal on

the plains and large quantities of it are canned. The mince-meat may be made by simply substituting the rabbit meat for beef in your favorite recipe. The following is an inexpensive recipe:

1 Cup of rabbit meat which has been parboiled in salted water and drained, then chopped finely.

1 Cup chopped apple.

½ Cup finely chopped suet.

½ Cup seeded raisins.

½ Cup currants.

1 Cup molasses or syrup.

2 Tablespoonfuls sugar.

1 Tablespoon cider, lemon juice, fruit juice or vinegar.

¼ Cup chopped watermelon pickles or green tomato pickles.

1 Teaspoon of cinnamon or nutmeg.

1 Teaspoon of salt.

½ Teaspoon cloves, mace or other spice.

Mix together all ingredients except the meat, add the meat broth and simmer for about 1 hour. Add the meat. Pour into jars, and sterilize. Remove and seal.

STEPS IN CANNING MEAT AND GAME

For all meat, poultry or game canning the following general instructions should be kept in mind.

1. Sterilize the jars, caps and rubbers.

2. Grade the meat for size.

3. Cut up into convenient portions for cooking or canning.

4. Sauté, fry or bake, broil or stew as desired. This step can be omitted if you are an experienced canner.

5. Pack in sterilized, hot jars or tin cans.

6. Add 1 level teaspoonful salt per quart of meat for seasoning if not already seasoned.

7. If glass jars put on rubber and seal, not too tight. Seal tin cans.

8. Process in boiling water or steam under pressure.

9. Remove, completely seal the jar.

10. Invert to cool and test the joint.

11. Label and store.

If you can in tin use the enamel or lacquered cans. A slight amount of water in the bottom of the jars of prepared meat will insure quicker sterilization of the air remaining in the jar. Where meat has been stewed the liquor can be poured into the jar for filling. If you use a steam-pressure cooker outfit of course the time of cooking will be much shorter than if you use a wash-boiler or some other homemade outfit. If you cook in boiling water we call that the water-bath method.

The following data will be of interest to those who contemplate canning meat.

Hog on foot—weight 500.

Liver, heart and a part of the ribs were eaten at the time of butchering, therefore, not canned. The remainder of the ribs canned six No. 3 cans:
Ham 18, No. 3 cans Shoulder 18, No. 3 cans Roast 18, No. 3 cans Sausage 26, No. 3 cans Hash 4, No. 3 cans Gravy (which is also called stock) 5, No. 3 cans   The sausage weighed 52 lbs. before it was

canned, making 2 lbs. to the can.

There were 200 lbs. of fat for lard. After it was rendered there were 176 lbs. of lard and 20 lbs. of cracklings.

TIME-TABLE FOR CANNING MEAT, POULTRY AND GAME

TIME TO STERILIZE PRODUCTS IF USING HOT WATER BATH OUTFIT AT 212°F IF USING WATER-SEAL OUTFIT AT 214°F IF USING STEAM PRESSURE 5 POUNDS IF USING PRESSURE COOKER 15 POUNDS PARTIALLY COOKED MEAT OF ALL KINDS
Roast beef
Corned beef
Sweetbreads
Tongue
Brains
Headcheese
Spareribs
Kidneys
Sausages and
other meats
Rabbits
Pigeon
Chicken
1½ hrs. 1 hr. 40 min. 30 min. UNCOOKED OR RAW MEAT Beef
Pork
Veal and all
other meats
Poultry and game
3 hrs. 3 hrs. 2 hrs. 1 hr. All meat stocks

with or without
vegetables and
cereals

1½ hrs. 75 min. 1 hr. 40 min.   NOTE.—This
time-table is for No. 2 and No. 3 tin cans or pint and
quart glass jars. If larger cans or jars are used more
time must be allowed for the sterilizing. If canning
in tin, scratch on the can at the time of sealing the
initial of the contents. For instance—S.R. means
spareribs; G. means goulash; R.B. means roast beef.
You can make out your list and mark accordingly.

CHAPTER VIII

FISH

People in some sections of the country are
interested in canning mountain trout and others live
where there is an abundant supply of either fresh-
water fish or salt-water fish. Heretofore we have
been wasteful and lax about the fish supply. But as
we have learned to can vegetables and meats so we
are going to learn to can fish. Fish is really canned
the same in every step after preparation as peas and
corn are canned.

In order to have a good product, fish must
be fresh when canned. No time should be lost in
handling the fish after being caught. Putrefaction
starts rapidly, and the fish must be handled
promptly. The sooner it is canned after being taken

from lake, stream or ocean, the better. Never attempt to can any fish that is stale.

PREPARATION OF FISH FOR CANNING

As soon as fish are caught it is advisable to kill them with a knife and allow the blood to run out. Scale fish. This is easily done if the fish is dipped in boiling water. For canning, most varieties of fish need not be skinned. If the fish is very large and coarse, the large back fin may be cut out and the backbone removed, but with most varieties this is unnecessary. Cut off the head and tail, being careful to leave no more meat than necessary on the parts removed. Remove the entrails and the dark membrane that in some fish (e.g., mullets) covers the abdominal cavity. Thoroughly clean the inside. The head may be cleaned and used for fish chowder.

If you wish to be sure that all blood is drawn out before canning, place the fish in a brine made of one ounce of salt to one quart of water. Allow the fish to soak from 10 minutes to 1 hour according to the thickness of the fish. Never use this brine but once. If the meat of the fish is very soft or loose, it may be hardened by soaking in a brine (strong enough to float an Irish potato) for from 15 minutes to an hour, depending on the thickness of the pieces and the softness of the flesh.

CANNING THE FISH

1. Remove the fish from the brine where it

has been placed in order to draw out all the blood and to harden the texture of the fish.

2. Drain well.

3. Cut into can lengths.

4. Place fish in a piece of cheesecloth or in a wire basket and blanch in *boiling water* from three to five minutes. Three minutes for the soft flesh fish, such as suckers, crappies, whitefish. Fish with a firmer flesh, as pike, muskalonge and sunfish require 5 minutes blanching. The blanching removes the strong fish flavor and cleans the outside of the fish.

5. Cold-dip the fish by plunging into cold water immediately. This makes the flesh firm.

6. Pack in hot jars or cans to within ½ inch from top. Add 1 teaspoonful salt per quart. Put on a good rubber and partially seal the jar, completely seal tin cans.

7. Place jars or cans in canner and process in *boiling* water for three hours. Three hours sterilization will insure the keeping of all varieties of fish, providing fresh products are used and the blanching and other work is carefully done. If canning with a steam-pressure canner or a pressure cooker sterilize for one hour and a half under 10 to 15 lbs. pressure.

8. At the end of the sterilizing period cool the jars quickly after sealing completely. The tin cans may be cooled by immersing them in cold water.

9. Store for future use.

SOFTENING OF BONES IN FISH

This can be done satisfactorily under pressure. The bones of fish are composed of large quantities of harmless lime, bound by a matrix of collagen, which is insoluble under ordinary conditions. When subjected to a high temperature under pressure this collagen is converted into gelatin and dissolved, leaving the bones soft and friable and even edible. Bony fish, such as herring and shad, which are too small to use otherwise are greatly improved when subjected to steam under pressure.

The bones in herring are softened in 37 minutes at a temperature of 240 degrees; shad in 1 hour; flounder 1 hour. Other fish are fully cooked and the bones softened in times approximately proportionate to the size of the bones.

The following table was made after many experiments and gives the time required to soften the bones in many common species of fish.

The term "softening" means the point in cooking when the small bones, ribs, etc., are soft, but when the large vertebrae are not yet sufficiently soft to be consumed along with the meat. In some of the larger fishes where the large bones could scarcely be eaten, even if they were softened, it would appear to be a waste of time and fuel to carry them to a point of complete cooking, and in such cases it ought to be sufficient to soften the small bones and sterilize the contents of the can. For such a purpose, the "softening" rather than the "soft" point, may be used.

The time periods are measured from the point when the given pressure and temperature are reached (at the top of the cooker) to the time when the heat is shut off. The heating-up and cooling-off period of time are therefore not included. The fish were salted, but no water was added.

Samples of fish canned during the course of these experiments were kept six weeks at room temperature (about 68° F.) and were then incubated at 98° F. for 48 hrs. All were sterile.

TIME REQUIRED TO SOFTEN THE BONES OF VARIOUS SPECIES OF FISH IN QUART JARS OR NO. 3 TIN CANS, 10 LBS. PRESSURE, 240° F.

WEIGHT
(LBS.) SOFTENING
(MINUTES) SOFT
(MINUTES) BLACK BASS Large
Small 5-6
¾ to 1 100
100 120
110 BLUEFISH Large
Small 6-9
1-2 90
80 100
90 BUTTERFISH Average ¼-½ 60 80 CATFISH Large
Small 1½-2
¾ 70
60 80
70 CERO Average 10-13 80 90 COD Large
Small 6-16
1-2 80
50 90
60 FLOUNDER Large
Small 1-1¾
½-1 70

50 80
60 HADDOCK Large
Small 3-5
1-2 60
50 70
60 HALIBUT Average 50-90 70 80 HICKORY
SHAD Average 1½-2 60 70 KINGFISH Average
½-1 60 70 LEMON SOLE Large
Small 2½-3½
¾-2 80
60 90
70 MACKEREL Average ¾-1½ 60 70
MACKEREL, SPANISH Average 1½-2½ 100 110
PERCH, WHITE Average ¼-¾ 100 110 PERCH,
YELLOW Average ¼-¾ 90 100 POLLACK
Average 5-7½ 60 70 SALMON Average 13-19 90
100 SEA BASS Average 1-1½ 60 70
SQUETEAGUE Large
Small 2½-4
¾-2 80
50 90
60 SMELTS Large, per lb.
Small, per lb. 5-7
15-20 60
50 70
60 SNAPPER, RED Large
Small 10-15
5-6 110
90 120
100 SUCKER Average ½-1½ 80 90 TILEFISH
Average 6-12 90 100 WHITING Average ½-1 50
60

FRIED FISH
1. Clean the fish and remove entrails. Split

along the back and remove backbone.

2. Place in brine strong enough to float an Irish potato. Allow fish to remain in this brine from 10 minutes to 1 hour according to the thickness of the flesh. This draws out the blood and hardens the meat.

3. Draw, wipe dry.

4. Cut in pieces that can go through jar or can openings.

5. Roll in cornmeal or other flour, dip into beaten egg and roll in flour again.

6. Then put into frying basket and fry in deep fat until nicely browned, or it can be sautéd in bacon or other fat until well browned.

7. Drain well by placing pieces on coarse paper to absorb excessive fat.

8. Pack into hot jars or enameled tin cans.

9. Add 1 teaspoonful salt per quart. Add no liquid.

10. Partially seal glass jars. Completely seal tin cans.

11. Process 3 hours in hot water bath outfit. Process 1½ hours in steam pressure (10 to 15 lbs. pressure).

12. Remove from canner. Seal glass jars. Cool quickly as possible.

BAKED FISH

Prepare and bake fish same as for table use until half done. Pack in hot jars, add salt and sterilize three hours in hot-water-bath outfit or 1½ hours in steam pressure or pressure cooker, 10 to 15 lbs. pressure.

ANOTHER FORMULA FOR
MISCELLANEOUS FISH

Rub the fish inside and out with a mixture made as follows: to 50 pounds fish, mix 2½ pounds salt, 2½ pounds brown sugar and 2½ ounces saltpeter. Let the fish stand in a cool place for 48 to 60 hours with the mixture on, then wash and drain. Fill into glass jars or enamel lined tin cans and add the following sauce until cans are nearly filled: ¼ pound whole black pepper, 1½ pounds salt, 1 pound of onions chopped fine, ½ ounce bay leaves, ¼ pound whole cloves, 2 quarts cider vinegar and 25 quarts of water. Soak the pepper, cloves and bay leaves for 48 hours in the vinegar. Put the water, salt and onions in a kettle. Bring to a boil and cook 30 minutes, then add the vinegar and spices. Let boil for one minute. Strain and it is ready for use.

Sterilize for 3 hours in hot-water-bath outfit.

Sterilize for 1½ hours in steam pressure or pressure cooker (10 to 15 lbs. pressure).

CANNED FISH IN OIL

Rub fish with salt, brown sugar and saltpeter as above directed. Wash and dry thoroughly in the sun. Spread on wire screens and dip in oil heated to a temperature of 300 degrees. Use a strap handle plunge thermometer to determine heat of oil. Cottonseed oil may be used for this purpose, although olive oil is best. As soon as the fish are cool enough to handle, pack tightly in cans, filling up with the hot oil.

Sterilize 3 hours in hot-water-bath-outfit;

1½ hours in steam pressure or pressure cooker (10 to 15 lbs.).

CANNED FISH IN TOMATO SAUCE

Handle same as specified under "Another Formula for Miscellaneous Fish," except pour in the following sauce instead of pepper, cloves, onions, etc.: Ten gallons of tomato pulp (mashed tomatoes and juice with cores, seeds and skins removed); 1 gallon cider vinegar, 1 pint Worcestershire sauce; 2½ pounds red sweet peppers; 2½ pounds sugar, 2 cups salt, 2 pounds onions (chopped fine); 1 pound West India peppers and 1 ounce Saigon cinnamon. The fish are processed same as "Fish in Oil." Enamel lined cans or glass jars must be used.

FISH CHOWDER

The cleaned heads of any fish, the backbones cut out of large fish with what meat adheres to them and all other fish scraps may be used for fish chowder. Put all these parts in cold water (to cover) and cook until all the meat can be easily removed from the bones. Pick all the meat from the bones, strain the fish liquor and return it with the picked fish meat to the kettle. Add the following ingredients: To every two pounds of fish picked from bones and the liquor in which fish was cooked add 6 onions, diced or sliced thin; 6 potatoes, diced or sliced thin; 2 tablespoonfuls fat; 1 teaspoonful paprika; 2 teaspoonfuls salt or salt to taste.

Cook vegetables, fat and seasonings until vegetables are half done. Pack hot in cans and sterilize same as all other fish. When the chowder is opened, heat and add milk according to taste.

FISH ROE

For canning be sure to use roe of freshly caught fish and only such roe as is known to be good to eat. The roe of some fishes, such as the garfish, is not eaten.

Clean the roe by removing the shreds and strings adhering to it and wash well in cold water, being careful not to break the roe. Soak for 2 hours in a brine made of 6 quarts of water and 6 ounces of salt. Drain and pack in hot glass jars or enameled tin cans. Can for the same length of time as other fish.

OYSTERS

Be sure all oysters that are to be canned are absolutely fresh, have not "soured" and contain no spoiled oysters. Oysters are opened by hand. All oysters should be rejected that have partly open shells, as this is a sign that the oyster is dead and consequently not fit to eat.

Rinse the oysters to prevent any pieces of shell or grit from getting into the cans. Blanch 5 minutes. Cold-dip. If the canned oysters are to be sold it is required by law to mark on each can the net weight of solids or meat exclusive of liquids.

There have been a number of standard

grades of oysters recognized on the Baltimore market. They are given as follows: "Standard Oysters" (four kinds).

No. 1 cans, containing respectively 1½, 3, 4 and 5 ounces of meat, after being processed in the cans.

No. 2 cans, containing respectively 3, 6, 8 and 10 ounces of meat.

"Select" and "Extra Select" Oysters contain respectively 6 ounces and 12 ounces for No. 1 and No. 2 cans. The above are the net weights of meats only that have been drained over a strainer with a wire bottom of ½ inch mesh. These are the only grades that have so far been recognized by the trade. An even balance scale, with one platform for graduated weights and another for articles to be weighed, is used to weigh oysters or clams. It is suggested that those who are going to can clams or oysters find out from their prospective customers just what requirements are as to weights and then make their pack meet the occasion. Under no circumstances is it advisable to make any misstatements or misbrand in any respect.

After oysters have been packed in the can, fill with boiling brine made of 5 quarts of water to ¼ lb. salt to within ½ inch from top of can. Sterilize as other fish.

CLAMS

If clams are received in a muddy condition, it is advisable, though not necessary to wash them before opening. After opening, discard broken or discolored clams. Do not can any clams unless absolutely fresh. Blanch. Cold-dip. Weigh out the amount of solid meat, after draining, that is to go into each can. Weigh and label just as oysters are weighed and labeled.

Fill can to within ½ inch from the top with boiling brine made of 5 gallons of water and 1 pound of salt. Sterilize.

CLAM BROTH AND CHOWDER

Place the clams, after being opened, in a kettle with enough cold water to cover. Add a few stalks of celery. Boil for 10 minutes. Season with salt, and pepper to taste and add 1 tablespoon butter to every 50 or 60 large clams. Can. Clam chowder can be made according to any recipe and then canned.

SHRIMPS

Shrimps when first caught are a grayish white color. They are very delicate and spoil quickly if allowed to stand for any length of time in a warm place. There are two general methods of canning shrimp—the "dry pack" and "wet pack." Nearly all the trade now calls for "wet pack" because the other always has a rather offensive odor and the meat is never so fresh and sweet of flavor as the "wet pack." Canned shrimp is very pleasing to the taste and is preferred by many to lobster for salads and stews.

Wet Pack. Medium sizes are preferable as very large shrimps are apt to be too tough and too dry. Put the shrimps into a wire scalding basket and lower into a boiling hot salt water solution made by mixing one pound of salt to each gallon of water. Allow the shrimps to remain in this bath for about five minutes, then remove and drain thoroughly.

Peel and remove viscera (entrails). The boiling and the salt will harden the meat and make the peeling comparatively easy. Pack into enameled tin cans or glass jars. Nos. 1 and 1½ cans are used almost exclusively. These sizes should contain 4½ oz and 9 ounces of meat respectively. It is unsafe to put in more meat than above directed, for it might cake and become solid when processed.

Add a very mild brine to within ½ inch from top of can. For the brine use 1 teaspoonful salt to 1 quart of boiling water. Sterilize.

Dry Pack. Handle same as above, except do not pour into the cans any brine. The fish is packed in the cans and processed as follows without the addition of any liquor.

Drying of Shrimps. After shrimps are boiled and peeled they may be dried. Spread on a drier of any kind and dry at a temperature of from 110°F. to 150°F. When thoroughly dry pack in dry clean glass jars or in parchment-paper lined boxes.

SALMON

Scale fish, clean and wipe dry. Do not wash. If the fish are large cut in lengths to fill the cans and in sizes to pass through can openings easily. Salmon is usually packed in No. 1 cans or in flat cans. Fill cans with fish after it has been blanched 5 minutes and cold dipped. Sterilize as other fish.

Many salmon packers lacquer the outside of their cans to prevent rusting. This is a very advisable point. The test for unsound salmon is the nose. If the contents issue an offensive odor, it is unsound. Freezing does not hurt canned salmon.

AMERICAN OR DOMESTIC SARDINES

The fish taught and used for packing domestic sardines belong to the herring family and are said to be of the same species as the sardines of France, Portugal and Spain. There are two methods generally used in canning sardines. First, when the fish are put in a sauce such as mustard dressing or tomato sauce, and secondly where they are packed in oil.

CANNING SARDINES IN SAUCE

The heads are cut off, the scales taken off and the fish cleaned. Blanch 5 minutes; cold dip; drain and pack into the cans dry. Cover with sauce, either mustard or tomato.

SARDINES IN OIL

The fish are prepared in the same manner as above described but instead of blanching them, they are put in wire baskets and immersed in boiling peanut or cottonseed oil until tender. Olive oil might be used, but is rather expensive. When cooked, they are drained, packed into cans in order, and the cans filled with olive oil. It is often advisable to salt the fish while fresh and before cooking as it improves the flavor.

CRAB MEAT

Put 5 gallons of water in a large kettle. Add ¼ lb. of baking soda to it. When boiling vigorously throw the live crabs in it and boil quickly for 20 minutes. Remove crabs and wash them in cold water. Pick out all meat. Wash the meat in a brine made of 1 ounce of salt dissolved in three quarts of water. Drain and pack in enameled No. 1 flat cans. Sterilize. As soon as the time of sterilizing is up, plunge the cans immediately into cold water, otherwise crab meat discolors. For this reason, glass jars are not so well adapted to crab meat canning as tin cans.

FLAKED CODFISH

The fish are first cleaned and the entrails removed, then the fins are cut off. The fish are then soaked for about two hours in a salt brine to remove the blood. This brine is made with about 10 lbs. of salt to 8 gallons of water. The brine is then rinsed off and the fish are cooked, either boiled or cooked by steam. When codfish are thoroughly cooked, the meat will drop off of the bone in pieces, and it is very white in color and crisp in texture. These pieces are then broken in suitable sizes and are ready to place in the cans. The cans are filled as full as possible, because after processing the fish will shrink some.

CRAWFISH

The best way to can crawfish is to put it up in a bouillon as follows: Water, 2 gallons; vinegar, 1 quart; cloves, 10; carrots in slices, 6; onions in slices, 6; cloves of garlic, 3.

To the above should be added a good quantity of pepper to suit the taste, a little salt and bunch of parsley and a little thyme. Boil slowly for about an hour. Throw in the crawfish after the intestines have been extracted; to do this take the live crawfish in your hand and tear off the wing which is in the middle of the tail; it will pull out at the same time a little black intestine which is very bitter. Boil one or two minutes, never longer, put in cans and process.

TIME-TABLE FOR BLANCHING AND STERILIZING FISH

PRODUCT NUMBER OF MINUTES TO STERILIZE SCALD OR BLANCH HOT WATER BATH OUTFIT 212°F CONDENSED STEAM OUTFIT 212°F WATER-SEAL OUTFIT 214°F STEAM PRESSURE 5 TO 10 POUNDS PRESSURE COOKER 10 POUNDS Fish of all kinds 3 to 5 min. 3 hrs. 3 hrs. 2½ hrs. 2 hrs. 1½ hrs. Shell fish of all kinds 3 min. 3 hrs. 3 hrs. 2½ hrs. 2 hrs. 1½ hrs.

CHAPTER IX

EASY METHODS OF CANNING IN TIN

If the proper sanitary requirements are provided and instructions of the cold-pack method of canning are followed, it is entirely safe and practical to use tin cans for all kinds of fruits, vegetables and other food products. Food poisoning—commonly called ptomaine poisoning—and the effects ascribed to "salts of tin" result from improper handling and improper preparation of the product before packing, or from allowing the product to stand in the tin after it has been opened. The raw food products used for canning in tin must be in sound condition, just as they must be if put into glass containers.

It is true that canned foods may be rendered unfit for use by improper handling of the product before packing and that decomposition may occur after canning, owing to insufficient processing, improper sealing or the use of leaky containers. This condition, however, is no more likely to be encountered in foods put up in tin than in products canned in other types of containers. You run no more danger of poison from your own tin-canned products than from tin-canned food bought at the store. Most canned foods if in a spoiled condition readily show this condition by the swelling of the can or by odor or taste. Canned foods showing such evidences of decomposition should not be used.

Certain foods which are high in protein,

such as meats, peas, beans and fish products, may undergo decomposition without making this condition obvious to the senses. It is essential, therefore, that the greatest care be taken to subject such products to proper preparation and ample processing. It should be remembered that canned foods, after opening the containers, should be treated as perishable products and should be handled with the same precautions that are applied when fresh products are being used.

ADVANTAGES OF CANS

Many housewives ask, "Why can in tin when we have always used glass jars?" There are many advantages in canning in tin which we can well consider. There is no breakage as in glass; you can handle the tin cans as carelessly as you choose and you will not hear a snap or crack indicating a lost jar. Furthermore, tin cans are easier to handle not only in canning but in storing.

The expense each year of new tin covers or new tin cans is no more than the purchase of new rubbers and the replacement of broken glass jars. Furthermore, one big advantage of tin over glass is that tin cans can be cooled quickly by plunging them into cold water immediately upon removal from the canner, and thus the cooking is stopped at the proper moment. The product is consequently better in form and flavor than when the cooking is prolonged, as it must be in glass jars. Many women like the large openings of cans because they can make better packs than when using narrow-necked jars.

If you do not care to bother with the soldering you can purchase a safe and simple device that will do the work for you. This device is called a tin-can sealer. With a sealer no soldering is necessary. Even an inexperienced person, by following directions carefully, can seal a can as well as an experienced one. The sealed cans look exactly like those purchased at the store. Two or three cans a minute can be sealed with this device.

This is the way to operate a can sealer: Prepare the fruits and vegetables as for any canning, following directions formerly given for cold-pack canning.

After the fruits or vegetables have been properly prepared, blanched and cold-dipped if necessary, place them in sanitary, solderless cans. Put water or sirup on, according to directions. Put the top on the can and place the can in the sealer.

Raise the can into the chunk by swinging the raising lever at the bottom of the machine against the frame. Turn the crank, rapidly at first, with the right hand, and at the same time push the seaming-roll lever very slowly with the left hand until it will go no farther. This is one of the most important steps in the use of the machine. Continue to give the crank several turns after the seaming-roll lever has gone as far as it will go. This completes the first operation or seam.

Continue turning the crank with the right hand, and with the left hand pull the seaming-roll lever until it will go no farther in this direction. After this has been done give the crank several more turns, and the second and final operation is complete. Bring the seaming-roll lever back to the middle position and remove the can. The can is then ready for sterilization.

Before sealing a new lot of cans or after changing for a different size of can, one or two of the cans about to be used should be tested for leaks. If this is done and the cans stand the test it will be unnecessary to test the remaining cans of that same lot. The following is a simple and safe test:

Put one tablespoon of water into an empty can and seal. Have on hand a vessel containing enough boiling water to cover the can. Set aside and, as soon as bubbles disappear from the surface, immerse the can in the hot water. This heats the water in the can and creates a pressure within the can. Keep the can under the surface for two minutes, and if by that time no bubbles rise from the can the can has been sealed air-tight.

ADJUSTING THE SEAMING ROLLS

If bubbles rise from the can the seam is not sufficiently tight. If this seam is not sufficiently tight the *second* seaming roll needs adjusting, provided the directions regarding seaming rolls given below have been observed. To set the rolls proceed as follows: Loosen the nut on the bottom of the seaming-roll pin. With a screw driver turn the seaming-roll pin counter clockwise—that is, from right to left. Turn very slightly and, while holding the seaming-roll pin with the screw driver in the left hand, tighten nut with the right hand, and test as before.

Occasionally it is well to compare the seam after the first operation with the sample can which is sent with the machine.

If seaming rolls cut into the can they are set too close, and the seaming-roll pin should be adjusted in the opposite direction from above.

After adjusting, always test cans as suggested above before canning. The seaming rolls are set before the machine leaves the factory and should not require adjusting for some time, but I have found that slight variations in cans may make adjusting necessary.

If for any reason the second seaming roll is brought into contact with the can before the first operation is complete it may injure the can seriously, thus preventing an air-tight seam.

If the first seaming roll is forced in too rapidly it may ruin the seam. Push the seaming-roll lever gently and steadily, while turning the crank with the right hand. This rolls the seam gradually. There is no danger from bringing in the second seaming roll too quickly if the first seaming roll has completed its work.

There are thus, as you see, two kinds of tin cans used in home canning: The sanitary or rim-seal can, which is used with a sealer, and the cap-and-hole can. The latter consists of a can, and a cover which carries a rim of solder and is fastened on the can by the application of heat.

The sanitary can has a cover a trifle larger than the diameter of the can, thus leaving the full diameter of the can open for filling. That part of the cover that comes into contact with the can is coated with a compound or fitted with a paper gasket or ring which makes a perfect seal when the cover is crimped on the can. Some mechanical device is necessary for sealing this can, and this is the sealer.

Cans may be had with inside enamel or plain

without any enamel. The following fruits and vegetables should be canned in enamel-lined cans: All berry fruits, cherries, plums, rhubarb, pumpkin, beets and squash. All highly colored products should be canned in enamel-lined cans to prevent the bleaching effect induced by their action upon the plain tin. Some prefer to can fish and meat in the enamel-lined cans. Other products not mentioned here may be canned in plain cans, since they are less expensive than the enamel-lined cans.

Covers are lined in two ways, with the paper gasket and the compound gasket. The compound gasket is merely a preparation, scarcely visible, applied to the under side of the cover and is not easily damaged by handling. The paper gasket is a ring placed on the under side of the cover and must be handled carefully. If the paper gasket becomes broken the cover must be discarded. To sterilize covers having the paper gasket, place them in the oven for a few minutes, but *do not wet them*, before sealing cans. Do not remove or handle paper gaskets.

When the cans are removed from the cooker the ends should be raised; this is caused by the pressure within. If they are not raised at the ends the cans should be carefully examined for defects. After the cans are sterilized they should be cooled off in water. This will cause the ends to collapse. If they do not collapse the reason is probably due to overfilling. It must be remembered that peas, beans and corn swell a certain amount after water is placed in the cans; therefore, in canning these vegetables the cans should be filled only to within a quarter of an inch of the top. If the pressure of the air from without will not cause the end to collapse, it should be forced in by hand.

THE TINNING OUTFIT

Tin-can sealers are made to handle the regular Number 2, or pint cans, and the Number 3, or quart cans. The sizes are interchangeable, so that in a few minutes' time a Number 2 machine may be changed into a Number 3 machine with the necessary attachments. So it is economy to buy a machine with these attachments, as you can then use either pints or quarts as you desire.

If you are selling to boarding houses and hotels you also will want half-gallon and gallon cans. If you use these larger-size cans and want the sealer you can get it for these sizes, but you must tell exactly what you want when ordering.

The prices which I give are 1919 prices and are of course not stationary. A sealer that will seal the Number 2 sanitary tin cans costs $14. A sealer for Number 3 cans will cost the same amount. But the ideal arrangement is the combination machine which can be used for both the pints, Number 2, and the quarts, Number 3. This type of sealer costs $16.50. A special machine is used for sealing the Number 10 or gallon cans, and its price is $35.

The price of the "winter can opener" is $17.00 for smaller size and $19.50 for the larger one.

Several standard sizes of tin cans are in common use for canning purposes, as follows:
NUMBER SIZE
INCHES DIAMETER OF
OPENING

INCHES 1 2⅝ by 4 2-1/16 2 3-5/16 by 4-9/16 2-1/16 or 2-7/16 3 4⅛ by 4⅞ 2-1/16 or 2-7/16 10 6-3/16 by 6⅞ 2-1/16 or 2-7/16 The cans are put up in crates holding 100 or 500 cans. If you are canning for the ordinary market use Number 2 cans for berries, corn, peas and cherries; Number 3 cans for tomatoes, peaches, apples, pears and sweet potatoes.

In buying cans it is always necessary to state whether you desire plain tin or lacquered—enameled—cans. In buying caps always ask for the solder-hemmed caps and give the diameter of the can opening. For whole fruits and vegetables, cans with two-and-seven-sixteenth-inch or even larger openings are preferable. Since the size of the can opening varies and it ordinarily will not be advisable to have more than one capping iron, it is recommended that the larger size—two-and-seven-sixteenth-inch—capping iron be purchased.

The tin cans come in lots of 100 or 500 cans. It is possible to buy as few as two dozen cans, but that never pays. It is cheaper to buy a larger quantity. Number 2 plain sanitary cans in 500 lots cost $3.45 a hundred; in 100 lots, $3.65 a hundred. Number 2 sanitary cans—enameled—in 500 lots cost $3.80 a hundred; in 100 lots, $3.95 a hundred. Number 3, plain, in 500 lots are $4.50 a hundred; Number 3, plain, in 100 lots are $4.70 a hundred. Number 3, enameled cans, in 500 lots, are $4.95 a hundred; Number 3, enameled cans, in 100 lots, are $5.10 a hundred.

The gallons come twelve cans to a case. They are $1.40 a dozen if 100 cases are bought. If less than 100 cases are ordered they are $1.50 a dozen.

The cans that you have to solder yourself run just about the same price, Number 2 being $3.60 in 500 lots and $3.80 in 100 lots. Number 3 are $4.70 in 500 lots and $4.90 in 100 lots. The buyer must pay express or freight charges on both sealers and tin cans.

PREPARING OLD CANS FOR REFILLING

Formerly, after using a tin can once we threw it away; but men with brains, realizing this waste, have come to our rescue, and as a consequence we can now use a can three times—that is, if we have a sealer. The sealer that seals our cans will also open them for us, so it becomes our winter can opener. With this can opener we can use our tin cans three times, buying each year only new tops, which cost less than good rubbers.

Cutting and Reflanging Tin Cans. Cutting off the can the first time. First lift the spring pin in the top piece, push the lever from you, drop the spring pin between the stop of the first operation roll and the cutting-roll stop. Place the can in the sealer, push the can-raising lever against opposite side of frame. Turn the crank and gently push seaming-roll handle from you until you come against cutting-roll stop, and the top of your can is cut off.

Reflanging. Remove standard can base and in its place put in the reflanging base, lift the spring-pin and bring seaming-roll lever to the original position. Drop the spring pin between the stops of the first and second operation rollers, place the can in the sealer, open end down, push raising lever round until the can engages with the chuck, turn the crank and at the same time gradually push raising lever round against the frame. The can is now ready for use again.

Resealing. The can is now three-sixteenths of an inch shorter than originally. Remove the reflanging base, put one of the narrow washers on the top of the can-raising lever, then the standard can base, and the sealer is now ready. Proceed as with the original can.

Cutting the Can the Second Time. Proceed as at the first time, only be sure to cut off the opposite end. The can may be cut open and reflanged only twice, once on each end of the can body. In cutting and reflanging the second time, leave the three-sixteenth-inch washer under the can base and reflanging base.

Resealing the Second Time. Remove reflanging base and put the second three-sixteenth-inch washer under the standard can base and proceed as directed under resealing.

THE SOLDERING OUTFIT

The soldering equipment required includes a capping iron, a tipping copper, soldering flux, a small brush, a porcelain, glass or stoneware cup in which to keep the soldering flux: sal ammoniac, a few scraps of zinc, solder, a soft brick and a file.

Soldering Flux. Soldering flux is a solution of zinc in crude muriatic acid. It is used for cleaning the irons and for brushing the tins and lead surfaces so as to make it possible for the melted lead to adhere to the tin.

To Make the Flux. Purchase at the drug store ten cents' worth of crude muriatic acid. Place this in a porcelain, stone or glass jar. Add as much zinc in small pieces as the acid will thoroughly dissolve. The flux is always best when it has stood from twelve to sixteen hours before using. Strain through a piece of cloth or muslin. Dilute with a little water, about half and half. This will make the soldering flux. When using keep the flux well mixed and free from dust and dirt.

Tinning Capping Iron. Purchase five or ten cents worth of sal ammoniac at the drug store; clean iron with file or knife. Mix a little solder with the sal ammoniac. Heat the capping iron hot enough so that it will melt the solder and convert it into a liquid. Place the iron in the vessel containing the mixture of sal ammoniac and solder. Rotate iron in the mixture until the soldering edge of the iron has become bright or thoroughly covered with the solder. All particles of smudge, burned material, and so forth, should be removed from the iron before tinning.

Tinning the Tipping Copper. The tipping copper is tinned in very much the same way as the iron. Sometimes it is desirable to file the tipping copper a bit so as to make it smooth and to correct the point. Heat the copper and rotate the tip of it in the mixture of sal ammoniac and lead until it has been covered with the melted lead and is bright as silver. The copper should be filed nearly to a sharp point.

Capping a Tin Can. Use one tin can for experimenting. By capping and tipping, heating the cap, and throwing it off and simply putting another cap on the same can, you can use this one can until you become proficient in capping.

When capping the full packs arrange the cans in rows upon the table while the capping and tipping irons are heating in the fire. Take a handful of solder-hemmed caps and place them on all cans ready to be capped. Place a finger on the vent hole, hold cap in place, and run the brush containing a small amount of flux evenly round the solder-hemmed cap with one stroke of the hand. Do this with all cans ready to be capped. Then take the capping iron from the fire. Insert in center the upright steel. Hold the capping iron above the cap until the center rod touches the cap and holds it in place. Then bring it down in contact with all four points of solder-hemmed cap and rotate back and forth about three strokes. Do not bear down on capping iron. A forward and back stroke of this kind, if properly applied, will perfectly solder the cap in place. Remove capping iron and inspect the joint.

If any pin-holes are found recap or repair with copper. It may be necessary to use a piece of wire lead or waste lead rim from a cap to add more lead to the broken or pinhole places of a cap.

Tipping a Tin Can. Take flux jar and brush. Dip brush lightly in flux and strike the vent hole a side stroke, lightly, with brush saturated with flux.

Use the waste solder-hemmed cap rim or wire solder. Place point of wire solder over vent hole. Place upon this the point of the hot, bright, tipping copper. Press down with a rotary motion. Remove quickly. A little practice will not only make this easy, but a smooth, perfect joint and filling will be the result. The cans are now ready for the canner. The handwork is all over, for the canner will do the rest.

Precautions. Do not fill tin cans too full. Leave a one-eighth to one-quarter inch space at the top of the can and see that the product does not touch the cover. If any of the product touches the cover the application of the hot iron produces steam, which may blow out the solder, making it impossible to seal the can.

RULES FOR STERILIZING

Remember all fruits and vegetables are prepared for tin cans exactly as they are for glass jars and the period of cooking or sterilizing is the same. The following rules will help to avoid difficulties in the operation of the various canning outfits:

For hot-water-bath outfits, whether homemade or commercial.

1. Support the cans off the bottom sufficiently to permit the circulation of water under and round the cans.

2. Have the water cover the tops of the cans by at least one inch. The heat and pressure must be equal on all parts of the cans.

3. Count time as soon as the water begins to jump over the entire surface. Keep it jumping.

4. On removing the cans throw them into a sink with running cold water or plunge them into a pail of cold water.

5. If the cans are laid on their sides the false bottom is not necessary.

For steam-pressure and pressure-cooker canners the following precautions should be observed:

1. Lower the inside crate until it rests on the bottom of the steam-pressure canners. In the case of the pressure cooker put the rack in the bottom of the cooker.

2. Have the water come to, but not above, the platform.

3. Tin cans can be piled one above the other.

4. When the canner has been filled fasten the opposite clamps moderately tight. When this has been done tighten each clamp fully.

5. Have the canner absolutely steam-tight.

6. Allow the pet cock to remain open until live steam blows from it.

7. Close the pet cock.

8. After the gauge registers the correct amount of pressure, begin counting the time.

9. Maintain a uniform pressure throughout the process.

10. When the process is completed allow the steam to escape gradually through the pet cock. You can lift the pet cock slowly, using a pencil or a knife. This can be done only with tin cans. If glass jars are used the canner must be cooled before opening the pet cock. Blowing the steam from the pet cock is likely to cause a loss of liquid from the partly sealed glass jars.

11. Throw the tin cans into cold water.

12. If tin cans bulge at both ends after they have been completely cooled, it indicates that they are spoiling and developing gas, due to bacteria spores or chemical action. These may be saved if

opened at once and resealed or resoldered and processed again for ten minutes.

The following table will help you in estimating how many cans of fruit and vegetables you will obtain from a bushel of product:

NUMBER OF CANS A BUSHEL FILLS

	NO. 2 CANS	NO. 3 CANS
Windfall apples	30	20
Standard peaches	25	18
Pears	45	30
Plums	45	30
Blackberries	50	30
Windfall oranges, sliced	22	15
Windfall oranges, whole	35	22
Tomatoes	22	15
Shelled Lima beans	50	30
String beans	30	20
Sweet corn	45	25
Peas, shelled	16	10

CHAPTER X

INTERMITTENT CANNING OR FRACTIONAL
STERILIZATION

In some parts of the United States,
particularly in the South, such vegetables as corn,
beans, peas, squash, spinach, pumpkin, etc., are
canned by what is known as the fractional
sterilization, or the so-called Three Days Process.

Southern canning experts have had trouble
with certain vegetables, such as those named, when
they canned these vegetables in the wash boiler by
the cold-pack or one period method. They say that
the climatic conditions are so different in the South
that what is possible in the North is not possible in
the South.

The vegetables are prepared, blanched, cold-
dipped and packed as in the cold-pack method and
the filled cans or jars are processed in the wash
boiler or other homemade outfit a given length of
time three successive days.

After each day's processing the cans should
be cooled quickly and set aside, until the next day.

The method is as follows:

Process or sterilize glass jars for the
required number of minutes on the first day, remove
from canner, push springs down tightly as you
remove the jar from the canner.

On the second day raise the springs, place
the jar in the canner, process or boil for the same
length of time as on the first day. Remove from the

canner and seal tightly. Set aside until the third day, when the process should be repeated.

For this canning a good spring-top jar is good, although the Mason jar type of top will serve for one year; after one year of use it is advisable to fit old Mason jars and similar types with new tops.

If using the screw-top jars, such as the Mason, do not disturb the seal at the second and third processing unless the rubber has blown out.

This method is only necessary when depending upon boiling water or condensed steam to do the work.

A steam-pressure canner or pressure cooker is used in the South and many other places to avoid bothering with vegetables three successive days.

The steam canner or pressure cooker soon pays for itself in time, energy, and fuel saved as the vegetables may be canned at high pressure in one processing.

The following time-tables are those used in the South and will tell you exactly how long to blanch and process all products. The preparation of vegetables and fruits is the same as in the one-period method, but the time of blanching and sterilizing differs as the time-table indicates.

TIME-TABLE FOR PRODUCTS IN GLASS

(Hot-Water Canner)

Tomatoes BLANCH 1 min. LIQUOR No water SIZE JAR Quart PROCESS OR BOIL 30 min. Tomatoes 1 min. No water Pint 25 min. String beans (very young and tender) 3-5 min. Brine[1] Quart 1 hr. 15 min. Sweet potatoes Cook ¾ done 2 tablespoonfuls water Quart 3 hrs. Sauerkraut Brine[1] Quart 40 min. Baby beets Cook ¾ done Hot water Quart 1 hr. 40 min. Baby beets Cook ¾ done Hot water Pint 1 hr. 20 min. Soup mixture Boil down thick Quart 1½ hrs. Apples 1 min. No. 1 sirup Quart 15 min. Berries 1 min. No. 1 sirup Quart 13 min. Figs No. 3 sirup Quart 30 min. Peaches 1-2 min. No. 2 sirup Quart 25 min. Pears 1 min. No. 3 sirup Quart 25-35 min. Cherries No. 3 sirup Quart 30 min.

[1] Brine is made of 2½ ounces (⅓ cup) of salt to 1 gallon of water.

To make sirups recommended, boil sugar and water together in proportions given below:

Sirup No. 1, use 14 ounces to 1 gallon water.

Sirup No. 2, use 1 pound 14 ounces to 1 gallon water.

Sirup No. 3, use 3 pounds 9 ounces to 1 gallon water.

One pint sugar is one pound.

TIME-TABLE FOR PRODUCTS IN GLASS

The following vegetables should be processed the same length of time on each of three successive days:

BLANCH LIQUOR SIZE JAR PROCESS OR BOIL ON EACH
OF THREE
SUCCESSIVE DAYS Corn 2 min. on cob Water,

salt and sugar Pint 1½ hr. Garden peas 1 to 4 min. Water, salt and sugar Quart 1½ hr. Asparagus 1 min. Brine[1] Pint 1 hr. and 20 min. Asparagus 1 min. Brine[1] Pint 1 hr. Lima beans 2 to 4 min. Brine[1] Pint 1 hr. and 25 min. Okra 3 min. Brine[1] Quart 1½ hr. Okra 3 min. Brine[1] Pint 1 hr. and 15 min. Squash Cook done Quart 1¾ hr. Squash Cook done Pint 1 hr. and 25 min. Pumpkin Cook done Quart 1¾ hr. Pumpkin Cook done Pint 1 hr. and 25 min. Spinach 4 min. Brine[1] Quart 1½ hr. Spinach 4 min. Brine[1] Pint 1 hr. and 15 min.

[1] Brine is made of 2½ ounces (⅓ cup) of salt to 1 gallon of water.

TIME-TABLE FOR PRODUCTS IN TIN

(Hot-Water Canner)

BLANCH LIQUOR NO. CAN EXHAUST MINUTES PROCESS
OR BOIL Tomatoes 1 min. No water 3 3 25 min. Tomatoes 1 min. No water 10 5 1 hr. String beans 3-5 min. Brine[1] 3 3 1 hr. String beans 3-5 min. Brine[1] 10 3 2 hrs. and 20 min. Sweet potatoes Cook ¾ done 2 tablespoonfuls water 3 3 3 hrs. Baby beets Cook ¾ done Brine[1] 3 3 1½ hrs. Soup mixture Boil down thick 2 3 1 hr. Apples 1 min. No. 3 sirup 3 3 8 min. Berries 1 min. No. 4 sirup 3 3 10 min. Berries 1 min. No. 4 sirup 10 3 32 min. Figs No. 4 sirup 2 3 25 min. Peaches 1 min. No. 4 sirup 3 3 20 min. Pears 1 min. No. 4 sirup 3 3 20 min. Pears 1 min. No. 4 sirup 10 3 35 min.

[1] Brine is made of 2½ ounces (⅓ cup) of salt to 1 gallon of water.

To make sirup recommended, boil sugar and water together in proportions given below.

Sirup No. 1, use 14 ounces to 1 gallon water.

Sirup No. 2, use 1 pound 14 ounces to 1 gallon water.

Sirup No. 3, use 3 pounds 9 ounces to 1 gallon water.

Sirup No. 4, use 5 pounds 8 ounces to 1 gallon water.

Sirup No. 5, use 6 pounds 13 ounces to 1 gallon water.

One pint sugar is one pound.

TIME-TABLE FOR PRODUCTS IN TIN

The following vegetables should be processed the same length of time on each of three successive days:

BLANCH LIQUOR NO. CAN EXHAUST MINUTES PROCESS OR BOIL ON EACH OF THREE SUCCESSIVE DAYS Corn 2 min. on cob Water, salt and sugar 2 10 1 hr. and 15 min. Garden peas 1 to 4 min. Water, salt and sugar 2 3 1 hr. and 15 min. Asparagus 1 min. Brine[1] 3 3 1 hr. Asparagus 1 min. Brine[1] 2 3 50 min. Lima beans 2 to 4 min. Brine[1] 2 3 1 hr. and 10 min. Okra 3 min. Brine[1] 3 3 1 hr. and 10 min. Okra 3 min. Brine[1] 2 3 50

min. Squash Cook soft and creamy 3 3 1½ hr.
Squash Cook soft and creamy 2 3 1 hr. and 10 min.
Pumpkin Cook soft and creamy 3 3 1½ hr.
Pumpkin Cook soft and creamy 3 3 1 hr. and 10
min. Spinach 4 min. Brine[1] 3 3 1 hr. and 15 min.
Spinach 4 min. Brine[1] 2 3 1 hr.

[1] Brine is made of 2½ ounces (⅓ cup) of salt to 1 gallon of water.

You will notice in the time-table for tin, that there is a column for "Exhausting." After the can is packed and capped it is placed in the canner of boiling water to within 1 inch of the top of the can where it remains the number of minutes, usually three, indicated on the time-table. This is done to force the air from the can through the little hole left open in the top, and is called exhausting. Cans that are not exhausted frequently bulge after processing and are looked upon with suspicion. Cans exhausted too long frequently cave in at the sides. The time-table should be used carefully and followed strictly in this part of the process. Tin cans do not require exhausting in the Northern and Western states.

TIME-TABLE FOR CANNING VEGETABLES
STEAM PRESSURE

VEGETABLE PROCESS,
MINUTES TEMPERATURE,
DEGREES
FAHRENHEIT PRESSURE
POUNDS Asparagus 30 240 10 String beans, No. 2 45 240 10 String beans, No. 3 55 240 10 Beets 30 228 5 Corn 80 250 15 Okra 30 240 10 Peas 45 240 10 Soup, concentrated vegetable 30 228 10

Spinach 30 228 15 Sweet potatoes 70 250 15
Corn, lima beans and peas should never be packed
in larger container than No. 2. Corn is cut from cob
after blanching.

The brine used is made of 2½ ounces salt to
1 gallon of water, except for asparagus, which
contains 4 ounces to 1 gallon.

Beets and rhubarb when packed in tin must
be put in enamel-lined cans.

Process pints as for No. 2 cans; quarts as for
No. 3 cans, adding 10 minutes to each period.

String beans when more mature should be
processed at 15 pounds pressure for 30 minutes for
No. 2, and 45 minutes for No. 3.

CHAPTER XI

WHY CANNED GOODS SPOIL

Every day brings letters to my desk saying,
"Why did my jars of vegetables lose water?" or,
"When I looked into my canner I saw all the
beautiful dark sirup in the bottom of the canner
instead of in the jars," or, "What shall I do, my beets
are all white?" etc., etc. In this chapter I am going
to try and tell you a few things you must and must
not do. A few "Do's" and "Don'ts" may help you a
little in your canning and food preserving.

I want to say right here that if you have
failures do not blame the method as we are always

so apt to do. Experts have worked long enough, carefully and thoroughly enough, to convince themselves and others that the cold-pack method and the intermittent method, which methods are employed for cooking the product in the jar, are sure, safe, reliable and efficient methods. So if your food spoils convince yourself it is not the method but something else. Spoilage is due to imperfect jars, imperfect rubbers, imperfect sealing of tin cans, careless blanching, insufficient cold dipping or poor sterilizing.

CAN-RUBBERS

Possibly your canning troubles are all due to using a poor grade of rubber rings. This is poor economy. Rubbers are apt to give more trouble than anything else to canners when using glass jars. Many of the rubbers sold are of a very poor quality, disintegrating quickly when subjected to heat and strain. My sister, canning in the hot climate of India, has more trouble with the rubber proposition than anything else.

You want good rubbers, are willing to pay for them, and here is what you should know about rubber rings.

The one-period, cold-pack method and the intermittent method of home canning require a rubber ring essentially different from that commonly used in the old hot-pack method of home canning. Investigation shows that many of the rings upon the market are unsuitable for these newer methods, being unable to withstand the long periods of boiling required in the canning of vegetables and meats.

Practical canning tests have indicated that rubber rings for use in this method should meet the following requirements:

Inside Diameter. The ring should fit closely, requiring a little stretching to get it around the neck of the jar. For standard jars the ring should have an inside diameter of 2¼ inches.

Width of Ring and Flange. The width of the ring or flange may vary from one-fourth of an inch to twelve thirty-seconds of an inch. Tests which have been made show that fewer cases of "blow-out" occur when the flange is ten thirty-seconds of an inch.

Thickness. Rubber rings as found on the market may vary from 1/18 to 1/10 of an inch in thickness. Tests show that 1/12 of an inch in thickness is sufficient to take up the unevenness in the jar and still not so thick as to make it difficult to place the cap or adjust the bail.

Cold-pack and intermittent-canning require a rubber ring that is tough, does not enlarge perceptibly when heated in water or steam, and is not forced out of position between the top and the jar by slight pressure within the jar. This we call a "blow-out."

Rubber rings should be capable of withstanding four hours of sterilization in boiling water without blowing out on partially sealed jars, or one hour under ten pounds of steam pressure. They should be selected with reference to proper inside diameter, width of flange, and thickness. Good rubber will stretch considerably and return promptly to place without changing the inside diameter. They should also be reasonably firm and able to stand without breakage. Color is given to rings by adding coloring matter during the manufacturing process. The color of the ring is no index to its usefulness in home canning. Red, white, black or gray may be used.

Always use *new* can-rubbers with each year's product of canned goods. An old rubber may look like a new one but it has lost its elasticity and its use may cause imperfect sealing and thus endanger the keeping quality of the food. This is always a hard thing to impress upon thrifty penny-saving housekeepers. The old rubber looks so good, so why not use it? But be wise in this and remember it is *never safe to use old rubbers*. New rubbers are expensive but what about the cost of the product, the loss of your time and fuel! One jar lost due to an old rubber is so much food, time and fuel lost.

And do not think yourself thrifty to use two old rubber rings instead of one, thereby thinking to obtain a better seal, for you will not. Two old rubbers are inferior in strength to one new good rubber. If you use old rubbers and your canned goods spoil, blame the rubbers.

GLASS JARS

Next in importance to the rubbers are the glass jars you use. There are many kinds of fruit jars on the market. The question is frequently asked, "Which jars on the market are the best." The only answer to that is to choose the jar which is simplest in construction, which will seal perfectly and wash easily, which protects the contained food against contact with metal, which has the fewest parts to

lose or misplace and which fits the shelves and
receptacles planned to hold it.

FLAT SOUR

Flat-sour often causes annoyance to
beginners in canning some vegetables, such as corn,
peas, beans and asparagus. These canned foods may
show no signs of spoilage and yet when the can is
opened the product may have a sour taste and a
disagreeable odor. This "flat-sour" is not harmful
and must not be confused with "botulinus," which is
harmful. However, the taste and odor are so
disagreeable you will have no desire to eat "flat-
sour" canned goods.

This trouble can be avoided if you will use
fresh products, that is, those which have not been
allowed to wilt or stand around the shops for
several days, and will blanch, cold-dip, and pack
one jar of product at a time, and place each jar in
the canner as it is packed. The first jars in will not
be affected by the extra cooking. When the steam-
pressure canner is used the jars or cans may be
placed in the retort and the cover placed into
position but not clamped down until the retort is
filled.

TROUBLES WITH CORN

Corn seems to give the most trouble, but
with a little care and study this product may be
canned as easily as any other grown in the garden.
A little experience in selecting the ears and ability

to recognize corn that is just between the milk and dough stage is important. Blanch not longer than five minutes. A plunge in cold water is sufficient. Cut the corn from the cob with a sharp knife and pack at once in sterilized jars. Best results can be accomplished when two people cut and one person fills. If it is necessary for one person to work alone, cut off sufficient corn to fill one jar, pour on *boiling* water, add salt, place rubber and cap in position and put the jar at once in the canner. A little overcooking does not injure the quality of canned corn. Corn should not be tightly packed in the jar; it expands a little in processing and for this reason each jar should be filled scant full. Corn that has a cheesy appearance after canning had reached the dough stage before being packed. Corn should never be allowed to remain in the cold dip and large quantities should not be dipped at one time unless sufficient help is available to handle the product quickly.

Some to be absolutely sure when canning corn, cook it for ten minutes in hot water before packing into jars.

Leave fully one inch of space at the top when packing corn but enough water may be poured into the jar to fill the can or jar, for when the corn swells the water will be absorbed.

Corn Turning Dark. A dark color in canned corn is due to some of the following causes:

1. Using water that contains too much iron.

2. Using corn that has reached the dough stage.

3. Blanching for too long a period—five minutes is sufficient for corn.

Water-Logged or Soaked Corn. When

canned corn becomes "water-logged" or "soaked" it is due to such causes as the following:

1. Allowing the product to stand in the cold water too long after the hot dip.

2. Allowing the jars to stand after they have been packed, and filled with boiling water. The jars should be immediately placed in the sterilizer after being packed.

3. Allowing ears of corn to stand in cold water after opening.

4. Heating corn in warm water over a slow fire.

BEETS, THEIR LOSS OF COLOR

The loss of color in canned beets is due to faulty methods of preparation before packing them into the jars. To secure good results 3 or 4 inches of the top and all of the tail should be left on while blanching. Beets should be blanched for five minutes and the skin should be scraped but not peeled. Beets should be packed whole if possible.

Small beets that run forty to a quart are less likely to fade and are the most suitable size for first-class packs. The older the beets the more chance there is for loss of color. Well-canned beets will show a slight loss of color when removed from the canner, but will brighten up in a few days.

CLOUDY PEAS

The condition of peas known as "cloudy" is due to such causes as the following:

1. Cracking the skin of the pea.

2. Blanching for too long a period.

3. Use of water which is too hard or has too much mineral content.

SHRINKAGE OF PRODUCT DURING CANNING

Shrinkage may be due to one or more of the following:

1. Improper blanching and cold-dipping.

2. Careless packing and using variety of sizes.

3. Sterilizing for too long a period.

4. Lack of sizing whole products for the container.

Sometimes there is a natural shrinkage that cannot be prevented. This is due to the fact that vegetables contain air in their tissues and when this air is driven off by the heat, the boiling water in the jar rushes in to fill its place. In consequence we have an apparent shrinkage in the amount of water. So be careful to do the blanching as correctly as possible to drive out the air; however, the product will keep just as well in a jar half full of water as if entirely covered with liquid. The contents of the jar whether food or air are sterile.

SHRINKAGE OF GREENS

Shrinkage of greens or pot herbs during the canning process is usually due to insufficient blanching. The proper way to blanch all greens or pot herbs is in a steamer or in a vessel improvised to do the blanching in live steam above the water line. If this is not done much of the mineral salts and volatile oil contents will be extracted by the water and lost.

LOSS OF LIQUID DURING CANNING

A loss of liquid in canning with a hot-water-bath outfit may be caused by one or more of the following:

1. Not having the water in the sterilizing vat cover the tops of the jars by at least one inch.

2. Not providing a suitable platform to hold the jars off the bottom of the sterilizing vat, permitting circulation of water under as well as around the jars.

3. Not having the wire bail that goes over the glass tops of jars sufficiently tight.

REASONS WHY JUICES ARE DRAWN FROM JARS WHEN CANNING WITH STEAM PRESSURE

1. Open pet cock after pointer or gauge has reached zero; test for pressure by opening pet cock slowly at first. The gauge does not register pressure until about one pound of pressure has formed, hence opening the pet cock before the pointer is at zero means that from one to two pounds of pressure is being relieved and this will draw the juices the same as allowing the boiler to stand and a vacuum to form.

2. Allowing the pressure to fluctuate during

the time of sterilizing, such as running the pressure up to fifteen, back to seven or eight and then up again.

3. Wire bails can be and should be a little tighter when jars are put in a steam pressure canner. The clamp should be left up as stated.

4. There may be an escape of steam around the seal of the boiler and this would allow the pressure on the inside of the boiler to fluctuate.

Any one of those four things will always cause loss of juice.

OPERATION OF HOT-WATER-BATH OUTFIT

These four rules will help in the operation of the hot-water-bath canning outfit: Example, wash boiler.

1. Support the jars off the bottom sufficiently to permit the circulation of water under and around the jars.

2. Have the water cover the tops of the jars by at least one inch. The heat and pressure must be equal on all parts of the jars.

3. Count time as soon as the water begins to *jump* over the entire surface. Keep it jumping.

4. Remove jars from the water and tighten the covers as soon as the time is up.

Rapid cooling of the products prevents overcooking, clarifies the liquid and preserves the shape and texture.

Operation of steamers or "double-deckers" as they are sometimes called. These have a small amount of water in a pan below two racks and the products cook in steam instead of boiling water.

1. Have water boiling in pan when products are put in.

2. Use same time-table as for hot-water bath or wash boiler.

3. Remove jars from steam at the end of the sterilizing period. Do not allow them to "cool off" in the steamer.

The operation of a water-seal canner is very simple.

1. Jars put on racks and lowered in water as in wash-boiler but due to an extra jacket the temperature is higher than boiling water.

2. Follow time-table under water-seal.

OPERATION OF STEAM PRESSURE AND PRESSURE COOKER CANNER

1. Place each jar in the canner as soon as it is packed.

2. Have water come up to but not above the platform.

3. Have canner absolutely steam tight.

4. When canner has been filled fasten opposite clamps moderately tight. When this has been done tighten each clamp fully.

5. Allow pet cock to remain open until live steam blows from it.

6. Close pet cock.

7. Force pressure to the required point before counting time.

8. Maintain a uniform pressure during the sterilizing period.

9. Allow canner to cool before opening pet

cock.

10. Have pet cock completely closed during the cooling.

11. Open pet cock before vacuum forms. This is evidenced by a rush of air into the canner when the pet cock is open. You can test this by placing the finger over the end of the pet cock. If a vacuum forms it will draw the flesh of the finger into the opening.

12. Remove jars from canner and tighten lids as soon as canner is opened.

BREAKAGE OF JARS

When breakage of jars occurs it is due to such causes as these:

1. Overpacking jars. Corn, pumpkin and sweet potatoes swell or expand in processing. Do not quite fill jars with these products.

2. Placing cold jars in hot water or vice versa. As soon as jars are filled with hot sirup or hot water, place immediately in the canner.

3. Having the wire bail of glass top jars too tight.

4. In steam canner, having too much water in the canner. The water should not come above the tray.

5. Cold draft striking the jars when they are removed from the canner.

6. Wire spring too tight, thus breaking jar when contents expand.

MOLD ON CANNED PRODUCTS

Mold may result from one or more of the following:

1. Leaky rubbers or defective joints.

2. Removing tops from the jars at the end of sterilizing period and substituting new rubbers, without returning the jars to the canning outfit for at least a few minutes.

3. If the jars are kept in a damp cellar where the rubbers may decompose, mold may enter through these decomposed rubbers.

ACIDITY OF TOMATOES AFTER CANNING

Too great a degree of acidity in canned tomatoes may be due to climatic conditions or overripe or underripe product. Such acidity can be corrected by adding ¼ teaspoonful of baking soda to one quart of tomatoes.

WATER REQUIREMENTS FOR HOME CANNING

The hardening of beans, peas and some other products after cooking or processing, or the turning of green vegetables to a dark or russet color usually indicates that the water contains too high a percentage of mineral matter. Water used for canning purposes should be pure, soft if possible or as free from objectionable and excessive qualities of mineral matter as possible. If you are to can any large quantity of food products and have difficulty with the water available, it would be well for you to have the water analyzed and for you to secure the advice of some one at your college of agriculture.

TOO MUCH SALT IN CANNED GOODS INJURIOUS TO QUALITY

Most vegetables as well as meats are injured in quality by an excessive use of salt for seasoning in the canning process. A little salt is very palatable and its use should be encouraged but it is better to add no salt in canning than to use too much, as it can be added to suit the taste when served.

ALTITUDE AND ITS EFFECT ON CANNING

Remember that practically all instructions on home canning are based upon a time schedule for sterilization from sea level to an altitude of 500 feet above sea level. When canning at an altitude of more than 500 feet above sea level, it will be necessary to use your judgment in the increase of time for sterilizing on the basis of 20 per cent for each 4,000 feet.

Blanching means *boiling*, not hot. In different directions for canning we often find "hot" water mentioned when boiling water is intended. Water should be *boiling at a gallop* when vegetables are blanched—berries and soft fruits are not usually blanched, though some are scalded to loosen the skin.

BERRIES OR FRUIT RISING TO THE TOP

Some women are disturbed because berries and fruits have a tendency to always rise to the top of the jar leaving a sirup space in the bottom. To prevent this you can scald all berries and fruits which are not ordinarily scalded, for one minute and then cold-dip them. They will be softened some, but remain firm, and can be packed very closely in a jar. They can be packed so closely that only a little sirup can be added. When a jar thus packed comes from the sterilizer the berries or fruit are not floating as they would be if they were not scalded.

Another method employed to prevent berries from floating is to put the hot sterilized jar on its side while cooling and to roll it frequently during the cooling period. The berries are then evenly distributed through the sirup.

In canning mushrooms in tin, always use lacquered cans. Do not fail to blanch and cold dip before packing, and remove the mushrooms immediately after opening the tin cans.

In canning cabbage and other similar products always soak the product in cold brine for one hour before sterilizing. Use ½ pound salt to 12 quarts water. This is believed to improve the flavor. Always wash greens or other vegetables, to remove all dirt and grit.

TROUBLES WITH TIN CANS

To discover pin-holes or any leaks in a tin can, immerse it in boiling water after sealing and if there is any bubbling from the can, you may rest assured it needs resealing.

Swells in tin cans are caused by insufficient sterilization. The action of bacteria causes gas to form in the can and as a result there is a bulging at either end. If left alone long enough the cans will explode. Watch carefully all bulging cans and use them first. Sometimes a slight bulge occurs when a can has been filled too full.

If you have trouble sealing tin cans the chances are that the can is too full. See that no particle of food touches the top or when soldering, if you employ that method of sealing, small pin holes will be blown in the seal by escaping steam which is generated by the hot sealer coming in contact with the cold food. Another cause of sealing trouble lies sometimes in a poorly heated capping steel or because it is not kept brightly tinned. To make a proper seal the steel must be kept bright, hot and clean.

Also, be sure you buy good solder as there are inferior grades that are too poor to flow when properly heated.

FROZEN PRODUCTS

Watch all jars and cans that have been subjected to a freeze. If the cans or jars do not burst the only harm done is a slight softening of the food tissues. In glass jars after freezing there is sometimes a small crack left which will admit air and consequently bacteria.

Sometimes cans and jars tip over in the wash boiler during sterilizing. This is caused by using a false-bottom which is too low or because it is not well perforated. Or it may be due to the fact that the jar was not well packed and so may be too light in weight.

CHAPTER XII

GETTING READY TO DRY

For various reasons women have not taken so kindly to drying fruits and vegetables as they have to canning these foods.

One woman said to me: "I like the canning because I can come to a demonstration and see the whole process carried through from start to finish. The drying of strawberries cannot be completed in sixteen minutes as the canning is." And another woman said: "What I do not like about drying is having the stuff standing round the house somewhere for so many hours. I like to get things in the jars and out of sight."

These two objections seem to be expressed more than any other. And in addition there is a third objection to drying: "I want my prepared food ready to use on a minute's notice. I can quickly open a can of my fruit and vegetables and there it is ready. With my dried things I have to allow time for soaking and cooking." This we will have to admit is true. But what weight have these three arguments against the many advantages of drying?

When we study the history of food preservation we find that drying was practiced before canning, pickling or preserving. I know my grandmother successfully dried quantities of things.

Vegetable and fruit drying have been little practiced for a generation or more, though there have been some thrifty housekeepers who have clung to their dried corn, peas, beans and apples. A friend of mine says: "Why, dried corn has a much better, sweeter taste than your canned stuff. I would rather have one little dish of my delicious dried corn than two big dishes of your canned corn."

Drying, I think we will all admit, does not and cannot take the place of canning fruits and vegetables in glass or tin. Drying and canning are twin sisters, and always go hand in hand.

The ideal arrangement for all homes, whether on the farm, in the village, in the town or in the city, is to have an ample supply of canned food for emergencies and quick service, and an equally ample supply of dried foods when meals are planned beforehand and there is time enough for the soaking and cooking of the dried foods.

THE ADVANTAGES OF DRYING

When we come right down to facts, drying has many advantages over canning.

The process is very simple, as you will see. The cost is slight. In almost every home the necessary equipment, in its simplest form, is already at hand. There is no expense for glass jars or tin cans, and with ordinary care there is no loss of products, as there may be in handling glass jars or from spoilage. The actual work requires less time and less skill than canning and the dried products when properly prepared are just as good as the canned ones—some say better.

One special thing in favor of drying is the little storage space needed. You can often reduce 100 pounds of fresh product to ten pounds by drying, without any loss of food value and with little loss of flavor.

Dried products can be moved more conveniently than glass jars or tin cans, for they are usually reduced to from one-third to one-fifth of the original bulk.

Another valuable thing about drying is that the little odds and ends one would scarcely bother to can may be dried in the oven as you go about your housework.

I have often been asked the difference between the meaning of the terms "evaporated," "dried," "desiccated" and "dehydrated." These terms are used more or less interchangeably when applied to foods from which the moisture has been removed. In a general way, however, "evaporated" products are those from which the moisture has been removed through the agency of artificial heat; dried fruit is that which has been exposed to the heat of the sun, though not infrequently the term is applied to products handled in the evaporator. The other terms are commonly applied to products that have been evaporated by one of the various patented processes in which equipment of some special design has been used.

To avoid any confusion we will use the

general term "dried" for all products that have enough of the water removed to prevent bacterial action, but which still retain the maximum food value, color and flavor of the original product. And that is what we want to accomplish when we attempt to dry.

How are we to remove the water and still retain food value, color and flavor? There are three principal methods by which we can do this. First, by artificial heat. Drying by artificial heat is done in the oven or on top of a cookstove or range, in trays suspended on the stove or in a specially constructed dryer built at home or purchased.

Second, by the sun. Sun drying is done either out of doors in the sun, under glass in sun parlors, or the products are hung in the attic where the sun has free access.

Third, satisfactory drying may be done by an air blast from an electric fan.

Of course any one of these may be used alone or two different methods may be combined. You can start a product on the stove and finish it in the sun, or *vice versa*.

The simplest and yet the most effective drying may be done on plates or dishes placed in the oven. It may be done on the back of the kitchen stove with these same utensils while the oven is being used for baking. In this way left-overs and other bits of food may be dried with slight trouble while the stove is being used, and saved for winter use. This method is especially effective for sweet corn. A few sweet potatoes, apples or peas, or even a single turnip, may be dried and saved.

To keep the heat from being too great, when drying in the oven leave the oven door partly open.

For oven use, a simple tray may be made of galvanized-wire screen of convenient size, with the edges bent up for an inch or two on each side. At each corner this tray should have a leg an inch or two in length to hold it up from the bottom of the oven and permit circulation of air round the product.

Oven drying in a gas range is an effective method if the temperature is kept even. An oven thermometer is a great convenience, otherwise the temperature will have to be carefully watched and the burners turned as low as possible. It is economy in the end to purchase an oven thermometer, for then you can have the temperature just right. It is best to start the temperature at 110 degrees Fahrenheit and dry at 130 degrees. Never go over 150 degrees.

If you wish to dry in the oven over the kerosene stove, place soapstones over each burner to prevent the heat from becoming too intense. Turn the burners very low until the stones are thoroughly heated. You can turn off the burners completely after the desired temperature is reached and it will be maintained from the heat of the stones for five or six hours. If more time than that is required for the drying, it may be necessary to light the burners again before the end of the process. The products should be turned constantly, so that they may dry evenly.

When using any oven for drying you can cover the oven racks with cheesecloth and spread the products on them. Always have the racks two or three inches apart to allow free circulation of air.

An effective dryer for use over a stove or range may easily be made at home. For the frame

use strips of wood a half inch thick and two inches
wide. The trays or shelves are made of galvanized-
wire screen of small mesh tacked to the supports.
Separate trays sliding on strips attached to the
framework are desirable. This dryer may be
suspended from the ceiling over the kitchen stove or
range or over an oil, gasoline or gas stove, and it
may be used while cooking is being done. If an oil
stove is used there must be a tightly fitting tin or
galvanized-iron bottom to the dryer, to prevent the
fumes of the oil from reaching and passing through
the material which is to be dried. A bottom of this
kind may be easily attached to any dryer,
homemade or commercial. A framework crane
makes it possible for this dryer to be swung to one
side when not in use.

A larger kind of homemade stove dryer can
be made. This is a good size: base, 16 by 24 inches;
height, 36 inches. The lower part or supporting
framework, six inches high, is made of galvanized
sheet iron, slightly flaring toward the bottom, and
with two ventilating holes in each of the four sides.
The frame which rests on this base is made of strips
of wood one or one and a half inches wide. Wooden
strips, an inch and a quarter wide and three inches
apart, serve to brace the sides and furnish supports
for the trays.

In a dryer of the dimensions given there is
room for eight trays. The sides, top and back are of
galvanized-iron or tin sheets, tacked to the
framework, though thin strips of wood may be used
instead of the metal. Small hinges and a thumb latch
are provided for the door. Galvanized sheet iron,
with numerous small holes in it, is used for making
the bottom of the dryer. To prevent direct heat from

coming in contact with the product and also to distribute the heat by radiation, a piece of galvanized sheet iron is placed two inches above the bottom. This piece is three inches shorter and three inches narrower than the bottom and rests on two wires fastened to the sides.

The trays are made of wooden frames of one-inch strips, to which is tacked galvanized-wire screen. Each tray should be three inches shorter than the dryer and enough narrower to allow it to slide easily on the supports when being put in or taken out.

In placing the trays in the dryer push the lower one back as far as it will go, leaving a three-inch space in front. Place the next tray even with the front, leaving the space at the back. Alternate all the trays in this way to facilitate the circulation of the heated air. It is well to have a ventilating opening, six by two inches, in the top of the dryer to discharge moisture. The trays should be shifted during the drying process to procure uniformity of drying.

Several types of stove dryers are on the market. One of these has a series of trays in a framework, forming a compartment. This is placed on top of the stove. Another is a shallow metal box which is filled with water. This is really a water-bath dryer. This dryer or dehydrator can be used on either a gas or coal range. A thermometer is necessary in order to maintain the right temperature. The slices of vegetables or fruit are placed on the tray with the thermometer, and the dryer does the work.

Commercial dryers having their own furnaces may be bought at prices ranging from $24 to $120. Some of these, in the smaller sizes, may be bought without furnaces and used on top of the kitchen stove. The cost is from $16 upward.

Sun drying has much to recommend it. There is no expense for fuel, no thermometer is needed, and there is no danger of overheating the fruits or vegetables.

For sun drying of fruits and vegetables, the simplest way is to spread the slices or pieces on sheets of plain paper or lengths of muslin and expose them to the sun. Muslin is to be preferred if there is danger of sticking. Trays may be used instead of paper or muslin. Sun drying requires bright, hot days and a breeze. Once or twice a day the product should be turned or stirred and the dry pieces taken out. The drying product should be covered with cheesecloth tacked to a frame for protection from dust and flying insects. If trays are rested on supports placed in pans of water, the products will be protected from crawling insects. Care must be taken to provide protection from rain, dew and moths. During rains and just before sunset the products should be taken indoors.

To make a cheap tray for use in sun drying, take strips of wood three-quarters of an inch thick and two inches wide for the sides and ends. To form the bottom, laths should be nailed to these strips, with spaces of one-eighth of an inch between the laths to permit air circulation. A length of four feet, corresponding to the standard lengths of laths, is economical. Instead of the laths galvanized-wire screen with openings of one-eighth or one-quarter of an inch, may be used. In using wire the size of the tray should be regulated by the width of wire screen obtainable. The trays should be of uniform size, so that they may be stacked together for convenience in handling.

A small homemade sun dryer, easily constructed, is made of light strips of wood, a sheet of glass, a small amount of galvanized-wire screen and some cheesecloth. A convenient size for the glass top is eighteen by twenty-four inches. To hold the glass make a light wooden frame of strips of wood a half inch thick and one inch wide. This frame should have legs of material one by one and a half inches, with a length of twelve inches for the front legs and eighteen inches for those in the rear. This will cause the top to slope, which aids in circulation of air and gives direct exposure to the rays of the sun. As a tray support nail a strip of wood to the legs on each of the four sides, about four inches below the top framework and sloping parallel with the top. The tray is made of thin strips of wood about two inches wide and has a galvanized-wire screen bottom. There will be a space of about two inches between the top edges of the tray and the glass top of the dryer, to allow for circulation of air.

Protect both sides, the bottom and the front of the dryer with cheesecloth, tacked on securely and snugly, to exclude insects and dust without interfering with circulation. At the rear place a cheesecloth curtain, tacked at the top but swinging free below, to allow the tray to be moved in and out. Brace the bottom of this curtain with a thin strip of wood, as is done in window shades. This curtain is to be fastened to the legs by buttons when the tray is in place. If you have a sunny, breezy attic you can hang your drying trays there.

The use of an electric fan is an effective

means of drying. As there is no danger of the food scorching, the fan proves as effective as the sun for drying.

Sliced vegetables or fruits are placed on trays one foot wide and three feet long. These trays are stacked and the fan placed close to one end, with the current of air directed lengthwise along the trays. The number of trays to be used is regulated by the size of the fan. Drying by this process may be done in twenty-four hours or less. With sliced string beans and shredded sweet potatoes a few hours are sufficient if the air is dry.

Of importance equal to proper drying is the proper packing and storage of the finished product. Use baking-powder and coffee cans and similar covered tins, pasteboard boxes with tight-fitting covers, strong paper bags, and patented paraffin paper boxes, which may be bought in quantities at comparatively low cost.

A paraffin container of the type used by oyster dealers for the delivery of oysters will be found inexpensive and easily handled. If using this or a baking-powder can or similar container, after filling adjust the cover closely. The cover should then be sealed. To do this paste a strip of paper round the top of the can, covering the joint between can and cover for the purpose of excluding air. Pasteboard boxes should be sealed by applying melted paraffin with a brush to the joint.

If a paper bag is used the top should be twisted, doubled over and tied with a string. Moisture may be kept out of paper bags by coating them, using a brush dipped into melted paraffin. Another good precaution is to store bags in an ordinary lard pail or can or other tin vessel having a closely fitting cover.

The products should be stored in a cool, dry place, well ventilated and protected from rats, mice and insects. In localities where the air is very moist, moisture-proof containers must be used. It is good practice to use small containers, so that it will not be necessary to leave the contents exposed long after opening and before using.

A very good plan is to pack just enough fruit or vegetables for one or two meals in each container. This will lessen the chance of large quantities being spoiled. For convenience label all packages.

CHAPTER XIII

HOW TO DRY FRUITS

Having decided to add the accomplishment of drying to your other housewifely arts, you have given some thought and study to the subject of driers. You now know whether you prefer sun, artificial or fan drying. You have either made or bought some kind of a drier. Little other equipment is needed.

A few good paring knives, some plates, and if possible some cutting or slicing device to lighten the work of preparation are all that are necessary. A sharp kitchen knife will serve every purpose in slicing and cutting fruits for drying, if no other device is at hand. The thickness of all slices of fruit should be from an eighth to a quarter of an inch. Whether sliced or cut into strips the pieces should be small, so as to dry quickly. They should not, however, be so small as to make them hard to handle or to keep them from being used to advantage in preparing dishes for the table, such as would be prepared from fresh products. Berries are dried whole. Apples, quinces, peaches and pears dry better if cut into halves, rings or quarters.

Cleanliness is essential. A knife blade that is not bright and clean will discolor the product on which it is used.

Winter apples should be chosen for drying when possible, as sweet apples and early varieties are not so well adapted to the purpose. The Northern Spy, the Baldwin and the Ben Davis give a good-flavored dried product. Most early varieties lack sufficient firmness of texture for the best results. On the other hand, some comparatively early kinds, such as Gravenstein and Porter, are considerably prized in some sections.

To prepare them for drying, apples are peeled, cored, trimmed and sliced one quarter of an inch thick. Be sure to cut out all worm holes, decayed spots and other blemishes. Defects are easily cut out with an ordinary straight-back, sharp-pointed knife having a blade two and a half to three inches long.

To prevent discoloration, as fast as the fruit is prepared dip it into a weak salt solution—three level teaspoonfuls of salt to one gallon of water. After all the apples are prepared, remove surplus moisture and put on trays, water-bath drier or whatever device you are using.

HOW TO REGULATE THE HEAT

Start with the temperature at 110 degrees
Fahrenheit, gradually raise it to 130 degrees and do
the drying at that temperature. It is important to
know the degree of heat in the drier, and this cannot
be determined very accurately except by using a
thermometer. Inexpensive oven thermometers can
be bought or an ordinary thermometer can be
suspended in the drier. If a thermometer is not used
the greatest care should be given to the regulation
of the heat. The temperature in the drier rises rather
quickly and the product may scorch unless close
attention is given to it.

The reason sun drying is popularly believed
to give fruits and vegetables a sweeter flavor
probably is that in the sun they never are scorched,
whereas in the oven or over a stove scorching is
likely to happen unless one is very careful. An oven
or dairy thermometer is a good investment. If you
do not have a thermometer test the heat by the air
feeling warm to the hand. The product should never
be so hot that it cannot be grasped in the hand. In
order to prevent the fruit from burning where
artificial heat is used and to keep it from sticking to
the drier by remaining in contact with it too long,
stir the fruit occasionally. To insure the most
uniform drying in sun drying, the fruit also should
be stirred occasionally.

Remember that if trays with metal bottoms
are used for drying, they should be covered with
cheesecloth to prevent acid action. Oven racks may
be covered with either cheesecloth or heavy
wrapping paper.

The interval between stirring varies with the

type of drier used, with the condition of the fruit and with the degree of heat maintained. Make the first stirring within two hours after the drying is begun. After that examine the product from time to time and stir often enough to prevent scorching or sticking and to insure uniform drying. Use a wooden paddle for stirring. Where several trays or racks are placed one above the other, it is necessary to shift the trays from time to time, so the upper tray goes to the bottom and the bottom tray to the top.

The time necessary for drying fruit depends upon several factors: The type and construction of the drier; the depth to which the fruit is spread; the method of preparing, whether sliced, quartered or whole; the temperature maintained; and weather conditions, whether bright and sunny or cloudy and damp.

If the atmosphere is heavy and damp the drying is retarded. Under some conditions it is hardly possible thoroughly to dry fruit.

There is possibly no step in the entire drying process that requires better-trained judgment than the matter of knowing when the fruit is sufficiently dried. A little experience will soon teach this.

The fruit should be so dry that when a handful of slices is pressed together firmly into a ball the slices will be "springy" enough to separate at once upon being released from the hand. No fruit should have any visible moisture on the surface. As the dried apples, pears, peaches and apricots are handled they should feel soft and velvety to the touch and have a pliable texture. You do not want fruit so dry that it will rattle. If fruits are brittle you have dried them too much.

After the apples and all other fruits are dried

they must go through another process, called "conditioning." The best way to "condition" fruits is to place them in boxes or cans and pour them from one container into another once a day for three or four successive days. By doing this you mix the fruit thoroughly and give to the whole mass an even degree of moisture. Pieces that are too dry will absorb moisture from those that are too moist.

You may lose a whole bag or jar of dried products if you neglect the conditioning, for if one moist piece goes into that bag all is lost. Moisture breeds mold and mold means decay.

Ask yourself these questions: "Do I ever lose any dried products? Are my dried products when soaked and cooked as near like the original fruit as possible?" If you lose products and if your dried fruits are tasteless you had better start the conditioning process. For with this one step added to your drying you need lose no dried products, and you need not dry the fruits to the brittle stage, as you must of necessity do when you put them away immediately.

After you have poured the dried products back and forth every day for three or four days as an additional precaution, reheat the dried fruit to 140 degrees just long enough—about thirty minutes—to allow the heat to penetrate throughout the product.

Two kinds of moths stand out prominently among insects that attack dried fruits and vegetables. They are much more likely to get into the fruit during the process of drying than to find their way through boxes into the stored products. This applies particularly to drying in the sun. The Indian-meal moth is the most destructive of these insects. It is about three-eighths of an inch long and has a cloaked appearance, one-third gray and the rest copper-brown. The fig moth is about the same size, but dark, neutral gray. A minute, flattened chocolate-brown beetle usually accompanies these moths and does considerable damage. Both of the moths deposit their eggs on fruit when it is on the drying racks—usually at dusk or after dark, for these insects are not fond of daylight.

It takes from three to ten days for the eggs to hatch into whitish or pinkish grublike caterpillars, and from five to ten weeks from the laying of the eggs before more moths appear to lay another lot of eggs. A number of "broods" or generations are produced yearly, so if a few of these moth eggs are stored away on dried fruits or vegetables hundreds of caterpillars are produced and many pounds of valuable material may be destroyed during the winter if the products are stored in a warm room. Dried fruits stored in warm, dark bins or in sacks offer especially favorable places for the development of these destructive moths.

It is evident that the larger the package, the greater the chance of a few eggs doing much damage. Small cartons or containers confine the injury from these moths to small quantities of material; for if the containers are closed tightly the insects cannot easily escape from them and infest other packages which may not have been infested previously.

If you are drying by sun and the products are not thoroughly dry at night, finish the process on the stove. If you desire to carry it over to the next day screen the drying racks early in the evening and fasten down the cheesecloth. With these precautions and with proper storage, no danger ordinarily need be feared from these insects. The additional precaution of heating the dried product to 140 degrees for thirty minutes sterilizes it if already infested.

Though not necessary, tin cans or glass jars make good receptacles for storage of dried fruits or vegetables. Pasteboard boxes with tight covers, stout paper bags and patented paraffin paper cartons also afford ample protection for dried products when protected from insects and rodents. The dried products must be protected from outside moisture, and will keep best in a cool, dry, well-ventilated place. These conditions, however, are difficult to obtain in the more humid regions, and there moisture-tight containers should be used. If a small amount of dried product is put in each receptacle, just enough for one or two meals, it will not be necessary to open a container, the contents of which cannot be consumed in a short time. If a paper bag is used the upper part should be twisted into a neck, bent over and tied tightly with a string. A further precaution is to place the small bags in a tin container with a tightly fitting cover, such as an ordinary lard can. All bags should bear a label.

Pears and quinces usually are prepared and dried exactly as are apples. Pears are attractive when cut lengthwise into halves, with the stem and calyx removed but the core left in. Or they may be quartered. If sliced like apples the drying period is shortened.

Peaches usually are dried unpeeled, but they are better if peeled before drying. The first step in the preparation of peaches is to split them open to remove the pit. To do this, cut completely round the peach in the line of the suture with a sharp knife.

The cut must be complete, for tearing of the flesh will make the finished product less attractive. If the fruit is to be peeled the paring should be done before it is cut open to remove the pit.

To facilitate the removal of the skin, dip the peaches in a kettle of boiling water for one and a half minutes; then plunge directly into cold water, after which the skins can be easily slipped off. After the pit has been removed, lay on drier pit side up. The juice of the fruit will collect in the pit or "cup" and will add to the flavor and quality of the dried peaches. The peaches can be cut into smaller pieces if you wish to lessen the drying period.

Plums and apricots are not peeled, but are cut into halves, the pits removed and dried in the same way as peaches. Small, thin-fleshed varieties of plums are not suitable for drying.

When drying cherries always remove the stems. The pits may or may not be removed. The best product for later cooking or eating has the pit removed, though large quantities of juices are lost in the pitting unless you provide some way of saving and utilizing it.

A prune is simply a plum having certain qualities not possessed by all plums. All prunes are plums, but not all plums are prunes. The final test as to whether a plum is a prune is the ability to dry without fermenting with the pit still remaining in the fruit. If a plum cannot dry without fermentation unless the pit is removed, it is not a prune. Prunes for drying, like other fruits, should be fully ripe.

Prunes are merely washed and then dried without removing the pits. The fruit is dry when the skin is well shrunken. The texture should be firm but springy and pliable enough to yield readily when pressed in the hand. The drying should not be continued until the individual prunes rattle as they are brought in contact with one another in handling. Prunes must be conditioned before storing.

In drying, prunes shrink about two-thirds in weight—that is, for every three pounds of fresh fruit you get one pound of finished product.

Smaller fruits, such as red and black raspberries, blackberries, huckleberries, dewberries, strawberries and blueberries, are simply washed and then put to dry. Berries must not be dried too hard; if too much moisture is removed they will not resume their original form when soaked in water. But the material must be dried sufficiently or it will mold. Haven't you often tasted extremely seedy dried berries? They were dried until they rattled. Stop the drying as soon as the berries fail to stain the hand when pressed.

To obtain the most satisfactory results soft fruits should be only one layer deep on the drying trays.

Fruits contain about 80 to 95 per cent water and when dried sufficiently still retain from 15 to 20 per cent of water, so it is a good plan to weigh before and after drying. The product should lose from two-thirds to four-fifths of its weight.

STEPS IN FRUIT DRYING
1. Thoroughly cleanse the product.
2. Prepare the product by slicing and so on.
3. Spread on trays; put in oven or put on commercial drier.
4. Stir occasionally.
5. Shift trays.

6. Test for completeness of drying.

7. "Condition" for three or four days. Sweet fruits may contain more moisture without spoiling than those of low sugar content.

8. Heat to 140 degrees Fahrenheit for thirty minutes, to kill all insects.

9. Pack immediately in available receptacles.

10. Label and store.

FRUIT PASTES

Fruit pastes are delicious and can be dried.

1. Select, wash, prepare fruit.

2. Cook until soft; stir.

3. Add sugar to sweeten.

4. Continue cooking until very thick.

5. Spread out flat by spoonfuls on oiled paper.

6. Dry in slow oven; finish drying over kitchen range.

7. Turn from time to time like griddle cakes.

Nuts of all kinds can be dried in these cakes, which may be left whole or cut in strips with scissors.

CANDIED FRUITS AND VEGETABLES

1. Select product of uniform size and ripeness.

2. Wash; prepare in usual way.

3. Cut fruit in halves, quarters or smaller sections; cut vegetables in narrow strips two and a half inches long.

4. Drop in a sirup cooked until it spins a

thread. To prepare ginger sirup, add a few roots of ginger to the sirup.

    5. Cook until transparent.

    6. Drain.

    7. Dry in slow oven; Finish drying over kitchen range.

    8. Roll in granulated sugar. (May be omitted for fruits.)

    This method is recommended especially for candied apples, peaches, pears and carrots.

    In a properly constructed sun drier, all fruits will dry in from 3 to 12 hours, under normal summer conditions. Time depends on dryness of atmosphere, sunshine and wind. Products dried in a sun drier, no matter how crude, are superior to those dried in the open without protection of some kind. Products dry more rapidly in high altitudes than at sea level.

    Racks in oven can be used. Plates or platters can be used in oven. A stove drier hung over the stove can be used. A water-bath or other commercial drier can be used with the stove.

TIME-TABLE FOR DRYING FRUITS

PRODUCT PREPARATION ARTIFICIAL HEAT
TIME IN HOURS
TEMPERATURE
110° TO 130° F. FAN—NO HEAT
APPROXIMATE
TIME IN HOURS Apples Peel, core, trim and slice

¼" thick. Drop in salt solution, 3 level teaspoonfuls
to 1 gallon of water to prevent discoloration. 4-6
24-36 Apricots Remove pits, but do not peel. Cut
into halves and dry, "cup" side up. 4-6 24-36
Berries, All Kinds Wash; stem or hull. 4-5 24-36
Cherries Remove stems. Pit or not, as desired. If
pitted, save and utilize juice. 2-4 24-36 Pears Peel,
core, trim and slice ¼" thick. Or peel, cut in halves
lengthwise; remove stems and calyx. 4-6 24-36
Peaches Peel, remove stones; cut in halves or
smaller pieces. If in halves, lay pit or "cup" side up
to retain juice. 4-6 24-36 Plums Do not peel, but
remove pits. Cut in halves and dry, "cup" side up. 4-
6 24-36 Prunes Wash; do not pit. 5-7 24-36 Quinces
Peel, core, trim and slice ¼" thick. 4-6 24-36
Rhubarb Select young stems. Wash and cut into ½"
pieces, using very sharp knife. Do not remove skins,
so the rhubarb will retain pink color. 6-8 24-36

CHAPTER XIV

HOW TO DRY VEGETABLES

Vegetable drying is a little more
complicated than fruit drying, just as vegetable
canning is more complicated than fruit canning.
Blanching is an important part of the operation. It
makes vegetable drying satisfactory as well as easy
and simple, just as it makes vegetable canning

possible.

However, there is one difference between blanching vegetables for canning and blanching them for drying. After repeated experiments it has been found that for drying purposes it is best to blanch all vegetables in steam rather than in boiling water. In vegetable canning we blanch almost all vegetables in boiling water, usually steaming only the members of the "green" family.

So remember that for drying all vegetables are blanched in steam. To do this steaming you can use your ordinary household steamer, such as you use for steaming brown breads and suet puddings, or you can simply place a colander over boiling water in a kettle. Do not allow the colander to touch the water. If you are fortunate enough to possess a pressure cooker, steam the vegetables for drying in it.

Blanching is necessary for many reasons. It removes the strong flavors, objectionable to many people. Beans, cabbage, turnips and onions have too strong a flavor if dried without blanching. Furthermore, it starts the color to flowing, just as it does in canning. It removes the sticky coating round vegetables. Most vegetables have a protective covering to prevent evaporation. The removal of this covering by blanching facilitates drying. Blanching also relaxes the tissues, drives out the air and improves the capillary attraction, and as a result the drying is done in a much shorter period. Products dry less rapidly when the texture is firm and the tissue contains air.

Blanching checks the ripening processes. The ripening process is destroyed by heating and this is to be desired for drying purposes.

Blanching kills the cells and thus prevents the hay-like flavor so often noticed in unblanched products. It prevents changes after drying, which otherwise will occur unless the water content is reduced to about five per cent.

Thorough blanching makes the product absolutely sanitary; no insect eggs exist after blanching and cold-dipping.

There is one precaution that must be followed: Do not blanch too long. Blanching too long seems to break down the cell structure, so that the product cannot be restored to its original color, shape or size. Follow the blanching time-table for drying just as carefully as you follow the blanching time-table for canning.

After the blanching comes the cold-dip. For the benefit of new canning and drying enthusiasts, let me explain that by "cold-dip" we mean plunging the product immediately into a pan of very cold water or holding it under the cold-water faucet until the product is thoroughly cooled. Do not let the product stand in cold water, as it would then lose more food value and absorb too much water.

You can cold-dip the product without removing it from the colander, strainer or steamer in which it is steamed. Plunge the vessel containing the product into the cold water.

The cold-dipping checks the cooking, sets the coloring matter which was started to flowing in the blanching process, and it makes the product much easier to handle.

Let us now see just exactly what we must do when we want to dry sweet corn, more of which is dried than of any other vegetable. All other vegetables are dried in the same way as is corn, the only difference being in the length of the blanching and drying period.

All vegetables are prepared for drying just as they are prepared for table use. When drying corn select ears that are young and tender, and if possible freshly gathered. Products for drying should be in the same perfect condition as you have them for table use. If wilted and old it is not worth while drying them.

Remove the husks and the silk, and steam— on the cob—for fifteen minutes. This sets the milk, besides doing many other things which blanching by steam always does. After the steaming, cold-dip the corn, and then cut it from the cob, using a very sharp and flexible knife. Cut the grains fine, but only halfway down to the cob; scrape out the remainder of the grains, being careful not to scrape off any of the chaff next to the cob.

When field corn is used, the good, plump cooking stage is the proper degree of ripeness for satisfactory drying.

The corn should be thoroughly drained as this facilitates drying. You can easily remove all surface moisture by placing the corn between two towels and patting them.

It is now ready for drying. The corn may be dried in the sun, but if so, it is advisable first to dry it in the oven for ten or fifteen minutes and then finish the drying in the sun. Never attempt sun drying in moist weather. The corn may be dried by artificial heat, either on top of the stove or in the oven, using either plates, oven-racks properly covered, or any commercial dryer.

Work quickly after the blanching and cold-dipping and get the corn heated as quickly as possible in order to prevent souring. You get "flat-sour" often when canning if you do not work quickly enough, and you will get sour vegetables in drying if you work too slowly.

Where artificial heat is used begin at a lower temperature and gradually increase it. As the corn is drying, stir it from time to time and readjust the trays if necessary.

After the drying comes the test to determine whether or not the corn is sufficiently dry. Vegetables at this point differ from fruits. Fruits are dried only until leathery, whereas vegetables are dried until they are bone-dry. They must crackle and snap.

This test is sometimes used to see if the product is sufficiently dry: Put some of it in a covered glass jar with a crisp soda cracker and keep them there for a few hours. If the cracker loses its crispness and becomes soft and damp there is still too much moisture in the product and it should be dried a little longer to obtain the degree of dryness required.

After the corn is bone-dry it should, like all other vegetables and fruits, be conditioned. This means to pour them from one bag or box to another, once a day for three or four days. This enables you to notice any moisture that may be left in the dried food. Foods that show any traces of moisture should be returned to the drying tray for a short time.

Notice Lima beans particularly, as they require a longer conditioning period than most vegetables.

After the conditioning, in order to kill all insects and destroy all eggs, it is advisable to place the vegetables on trays and heat them in an oven for half an hour at a temperature of 140 degrees Fahrenheit. Store directly from the oven.

Dried vegetables are stored just as are dried fruits—in cans, cracked jars that cannot be used for canning, fiber containers, cheesecloth, paper bags or paraffin containers.

In storing your dried products keep in mind these things: Protection from moisture, insects, rats, mice, dust and light. If you observe all these things it is unnecessary to have air-tight containers.

All varieties of string beans can be dried, but only those fit for table use should be used. Old, stringy, tough beans will remain the same kind of beans when dried. There are two ways of preparing string, wax or snap beans for drying:

1. Wash; remove stem, tip and string. Cut or break into pieces one-half to one inch long; blanch three to ten minutes, according to age and freshness, in steam; cold-dip. Place on trays or dryer. If you have a vegetable slicer it can be used for slicing the beans.

2. Prepare as above, then blanch the whole beans. After cold-dipping, thread them on coarse, strong thread, making long "necklaces" of them; hang them above the stove or out of doors until dry.

Lima beans should be shelled from the pod and then blanched two to five minutes if young and tender. If larger and more mature blanch five to ten minutes.

Okra is blanched for three minutes. If the pods are young and small, dry them whole. Older pods should be cut into quarter-inch slices. Small tender pods are sometimes strung on stout thread and hung up to dry.

Peppers may be dried by splitting on one

side, removing the seed, drying in the air, and finishing the drying in the dryer at 130 degrees Fahrenheit. A more satisfactory method is to place peppers in a biscuit pan in the oven and heat until the skins blister; or to steam them until the skin softens, peel, split in half, take out seed, and dry at 110 to 130 degrees. In drying thick-fleshed peppers like the pimento, do not increase heat too quickly, but dry slowly and evenly.

Small varieties of red peppers may be spread in the sun until wilted and the drying finished in the dryer, or they may be dried entirely in the sun.

Peppers often are dried whole. If large they can be strung on thread; if small the whole plant can be hung up to dry.

Shell full-grown peas and blanch three to five minutes; cold-dip and then spread in a single layer on trays to dry.

When drying the very tender young sugar peas, use the pod also. Wash and cut in quarter-inch pieces. Blanch six minutes, cold-dip and remove surplus moisture before drying. When drying beets always select young, quickly grown, tender beets. Steam twenty to thirty minutes, or until the skin cracks. Dip in cold water, peel and slice into one-eighth to one-quarter inch slices. Then dry.

Carrots having a large, woody core should not be dried. Blanch six minutes; cold-dip. Carrots are often sliced lengthwise into pieces about one-eighth inch thick. Parsnips, kohl-rabi, celeriac and salsify are prepared in the same way as are carrots.

Onions should be held under water while peeling and slicing to avoid smarting of the eyes. They should be sliced into one-eighth to one-quarter inch slices. Blanch five minutes, cold-dip,

remove superfluous moisture and dry. Leeks are
handled as are onions.

Select well-developed heads of cabbage and
remove all loose outside leaves. Split the cabbage,
remove the hard, woody core and slice the
remainder of the head with a kraut slicer or cutter or
with a large, sharp knife. Blanch five to ten minutes
and cold-dip; dry.

Spinach and parsley should be carefully
washed. Steam, cold-dip and dry. If the spinach is
sliced the drying will be greatly facilitated. Beet
tops, Swiss chard and celery are prepared like
spinach.

Select sound, well-matured Irish potatoes.
Wash and boil or steam until nearly done. Peel and
pass through a meat grinder or a potato ricer.
Collect the shred in layers on a tray and dry until
brittle. If toasted slightly in an oven when dry, the
flavor is improved somewhat; or boil or steam until
nearly done, peel, cut into quarter-inch slices,
spread on trays, and dry until brittle. Peeling may be
omitted, but the product will be very much inferior
in flavor. Irish potatoes cannot be satisfactorily
dried unless they are first cooked; otherwise they
will discolor.

All root vegetables must be thoroughly
cleaned, otherwise an earthy flavor may cling to
them. One decayed root may seriously affect several
pots of vegetable soup.

GENERAL SUGGESTIONS

1. All vegetables should be completely dried
in from two to twenty-four hours.

2. Materials should be turned or stirred

several times to secure a uniform product.

    3. If heat is used guard against scorching. The door is left open if an oven is used; the temperature should be about 110 degrees at the beginning and usually should not exceed 130 degrees. Onions, string beans and peas will yellow at more than 140 degrees.

    4. A thermometer is essential to successful drying by artificial heat.

    5. It is impossible to give definite lengths of times for the completion of sun drying, as this varies not only with different products but with the weather. A sultry, rainy day is the worst for drying.

    6. Vegetables should be stone dry.

    7. Succulent vegetables and fruits contain from 80 to 95 per cent of water, and when dried sufficiently still retain from 15 to 20 per cent; so it is a good plan to weigh before and after drying as a check. The product should lose from two-thirds to four-fifths of its weight.

    8. Work rapidly to prevent souring of vegetables.

    9. Small vegetables, mature beans and peas and small onions may be dried whole. Larger vegetables should be cut up so as to expose more surface for drying.

    10. The slicing, cutting and shredding should be done before blanching, with the exception of corn, which is cut from the cob after blanching.

TIME-TABLE FOR DRYING VEGETABLES

PRODUCT PREPARATION BLANCHING BY

STEAM, TIME ON MINUTES ARTIFICIAL HEAT TEMPERATURE 110° TO 130° F. APPROXIMATE TIME IN HOURS FAN—NO HEAT APPROXIMATE TIME IN HOURS ASPARAGUS Wash and cut into pieces 2 to 4 4 to 8 12 to 24 BEANS, GREEN STRING Wash; remove stem, tip and string 3 to 10 2½ to 3 20 to 24 BEANS, WAX Wash; remove stem, tip and string; cut into pieces or dry whole 3 to 10 2 to 4 5 to 8 BEETS Leave skin on while steaming [1]20 to 30 2½ to 3 12 to 16 BRUSSELS SPROUTS Divide into small pieces 6 3 to 5 12 to 16 CABBAGE Remove all loose outside leaves; split cabbage and remove woody core; slice or shred 5 to 10 3 to 5 12 to 24 CARROTS Wash; slice lengthwise into pieces ⅛-inch thick 6 2½ to 3 20 to 24 CAULIFLOWER Clean; divide into small bunches 6 2 to 3 12 to 16 CELERY Wash carefully and remove leaves; slice 3 3 to 4 12 to 16 CELERIAC Clean; pare; slice into ⅛-inch pieces 6 2½ to 3 20 to 24 CORN, SWEET Blanch on cob. From 12 ears of corn you should obtain 1 pound dried corn 15 3 to 4 2 days KOHL-RABI Clean; pare; slice into ⅛-inch pieces 6 2½ to 3 8 to 12 LEEKS Cut into ½-inch strips 5 2½ to 3 8 to 12 LIMA BEANS (YOUNG) Shell 2 to 5 3 to 3½ 12 to 20 LIMA BEANS (OLD) Shell 5 to 10 3 to 3½ 12 to 20 MUSHROOMS Wash; cut into pieces 5 3 to 5 12 to 24 OKRA Dry young pods whole. Cut old pods in ¼-inch slices 3 2 to 3 12 to 20 ONIONS Remove outside papery covering; cut off tops and roots; slice thin 5 2½ to 3 12 to 18 PARSNIPS Clean; pare; cut into ½-inch slices 6 2½ to 3 20 to 24 PEAS Can be dried whole or put through grinder 3 to 5 3½ 12 to 20 PEPPERS Skin blistered in oven, steamed or sun-withered .. 3 to 4 24 POTATOES,

IRISH Cook and rice them .. 2½ 5 to 6
POTATOES, IRISH Cook and slice them ¼-inch
thick .. 6 12 to 20 POTATOES, SWEET Cook and
rice them .. 2½ 12 to 20 POTATOES, SWEET
Cook and slice them ¼-inch thick .. 6 12 to 20
PUMPKINS AND SQUASH Cut into ⅓-inch strips;
peel; remove seeds 3 3 to 4 16 SPINACH Wash
thoroughly; can be sliced 3 3 12 to 18 SALSIFY
Wash; cut into ½-inch slices 6 2½ to 3 20 to 24
SWISS CHARD Wash thoroughly; can be sliced 3
3 to 4 12 to 18 TOMATOES Wash; slice after
steaming to loosen skin 2 to 3 2½ to 3 12 to 16
TURNIPS Pare and slice thin 5 2½ to 3 12 to 18
  [1] Till skin cracks.
  In a properly constructed sun drier
vegetables will dry in from 3 to 12 hours under
normal summer conditions. Products dried in a sun
drier are superior to those dried in the open without
any protection. Products dry more quickly in high
altitudes than at sea level.

CHAPTER XV

EVERY STEP IN BRINING

  We have learned how to preserve fruit and
vegetables by canning and drying and now we are
going to learn another method to preserve foods, in
which salt is used. We use this salt method for
vegetables. It is not adapted to fruits. We may

pickle apples, pears and peaches, but we ferment, brine and dry-salt only vegetables.

This salt method is not a substitute for drying or canning, but just an additional method we may employ. Every thrifty housewife of to-day wants her shelves of canned foods, her boxes of dried foods and her crocks of salted foods. Each kind has its proper function to perform in the household. One cannot take the place of the other.

For women on the farm salting is a salvation. In busy seasons when canning and drying seem an impossibility, a great many vegetables can be saved by this method in a very short time. The labor required is very small, as no cooking is necessary. A good supply of salt is the one necessity.

Besides the saving of time, salting saves jars, which are absolutely necessary in canning. Old containers can be used if they are thoroughly cleansed. The vegetables can be put in any container, so long as it holds water and is not made of metal. Metal containers should not be used. Old kegs, butter and lard tubs if water-tight, stoneware jars or crocks, chipped preserve jars, glass jars with missing covers and covered enamel buckets can all be utilized. Avoid using tubs made of pitch or soft pine unless coated with melted paraffin, as they impart a flavor to the vegetables. Maple is the best.

THREE METHODS OF SALTING FOOD

There are three ways of preserving food by salting: First, fermentation with dry salting; second, fermentation in brine or brining; and third, salting without fermentation, or dry salting.

Dry Salting. Fermentation with dry salting consists in packing the material with a small amount of salt. No water is used, for the salt will extract the water from the vegetables and this forms a brine. This is the simplest process of all three and is used mostly for cabbage. To make sauerkraut proceed as follows: The outside green leaves of the cabbage should be removed, just as in preparing the head for boiling. Never use any decayed or bruised leaves. Quarter the heads and shred the cabbage very finely. There are shredding machines on the market, but if one is not available use a slaw cutter or a large sharp knife.

After the cabbage is shredded pack at once into a clean barrel, keg or tub, or into an earthenware crock holding four or five gallons. The smaller containers are recommended for household use. When packing distribute the salt as uniformly as possible, using one pound of salt to forty pounds of cabbage. Sprinkle a little salt in the container and put in a layer of three or four inches of shredded cabbage, then pack down with a wooden utensil like a potato masher. Repeat with salt, cabbage and packing until the container is full or the shredded cabbage is all used.

Press the cabbage down as tightly as possible and apply a cloth, and then a glazed plate or a board cover which will go inside the holder. If using a wooden cover select wood free from pitch, such as basswood. On top of this cover place stone, bricks or other weights—use flint or granite; avoid the use of limestone, sandstone or marble. These weights serve to keep vegetables beneath the surface of the liquid. The proportion of salt to food when fermenting with dry salt is a quarter pound of salt to ten pounds of food. Do not use more, for the product will taste too salty.

Allow fermentation to proceed for ten days or two weeks, if the room is warm. In a cellar or other cool place three to five weeks may be required. Skim off the film which forms when fermentation starts and repeat this daily if necessary to keep this film from becoming a scum. When gas bubbles cease to rise when you strike the side of the container, fermentation is complete. If there is a scum it should be removed.

As a final step pour very hot melted paraffin over the brine until it forms a layer from a quarter to a half-inch thick, to prevent the formation of the scum which occurs if the weather is warm or the storage place is not well cooled. The cabbage may be used as soon as the bubbles cease to rise. If scum forms and remains the cabbage will spoil. You may can the cabbage as soon as bubbles cease to rise and fermentation is complete. To can, fill jars, adjust rubbers and partly seal. Sterilize 120 minutes in hot-water bath, or 60 minutes in steam-pressure outfit at five to ten pounds pressure.

The vital factor in preserving the material by this method is the lactic acid which develops in fermentation.

If the vegetables are covered with a very strong brine or are packed with a fairly large amount of salt, lactic acid fermentation and also the growth of other forms of bacteria and molds are prevented. This method of preservation is especially applicable to those vegetables which contain so little sugar that sufficient lactic acid cannot be formed by bacterial action to insure their preservation.

In the well-known method of vinegar pickling the acetic acid of the vinegar acts as a preservative like the lactic acid produced by fermentation. Sometimes brining precedes pickling in vinegar, and often the pickling is modified by the addition of sugar and spices, which add flavor as well as helping to preserve the fruit or vegetables. In some cases olive oil or some other table oil is added to the vinegar, as in the making of oil cucumber pickles.

Besides sauerkraut, string beans, beet tops, turnip tops, greens, kale and dandelions are adapted for fermentation with dry salting. String beans should be young, tender and not overgrown. Remove the tip ends and strings; cut or break into pieces about two inches long. Wash the beet and turnip tops as well as all greens, in order to remove dirt and grit. Weigh all products that are to be salted.

For salting, a supply of ordinary fine salt, which can be purchased in bulk for about two cents a pound, is most satisfactory for general use. Table salt will do very well, but it is rather expensive if large quantities of vegetables are to be preserved. The rather coarse salt—known in the trade as "ground alum salt"—which is used in freezing ice cream can be used. Rock salt because of its coarseness and impurities should not be used.

A weight must be used. The size of the weight depends on the quantity of material being preserved. For a five-gallon keg a weight of ten pounds will be sufficient, but if a larger barrel is used a heavier weight will be needed. The weight should be sufficient to extract the juices to form a brine, which will cover the top in about twenty-four hours. If a brine does not form it may be necessary to add more stones after the material has stood a while.

There always will be more or less bubbling and foaming of the brine during the first stages of fermentation. After this ceases a thin film will appear which will rapidly spread over the whole surface and quickly develop into a heavy, folded membrane. This scum is a growth of yeast-like organisms which feed upon the acid formed by fermentation. If allowed to grow undisturbed it will eventually destroy all the acid and the fermented material will spoil. To prevent mold from forming it is necessary to exclude the air from the surface of the brine.

Perhaps the best method is to cover the surface—over the board and round the weight—with very hot, melted paraffin. If the paraffin is hot enough to make the brine boil when poured in, the paraffin will form a smooth, even layer before hardening. Upon solidifying, it forms an air-tight seal. Oils, such as cottonseed oil or the tasteless liquid petroleum, may also be used for this purpose. As a measure of safety with crocks, it is advisable to cover the top with a cloth soaked in melted paraffin. Put the cover in place before the paraffin hardens.

After sealing with paraffin the containers should be set where they will not be disturbed until the contents are to be used. Any attempt to remove them from one place to another may break the paraffin seal and necessitate resealing.

Some vegetables which do not contain sufficient water are better fermented by covering them with a weak brine. Those which are the most satisfactory when fermented in this way are cucumbers, string beans, green tomatoes, beets, beet tops, turnip tops, corn and green peas. The general directions for this brining are as follows:

Wash the vegetables, drain off the surplus water and pack them in a keg, crock, or other utensil until it is nearly full—within about three inches of the top of the vessel. Prepare a weak brine as follows: To each gallon of water used add one-half pint of vinegar and three-fourths of a cup of salt and stir until the salt is entirely dissolved. The vinegar is used primarily to keep down the growth of injurious bacteria until the lactic-acid ferment starts, but it also adds to the flavor. Spices may be added if desired.

The amount of brine necessary to cover the vegetables will be equal to about one-half the volume of the material to be fermented. For example, if a five-gallon keg is to be packed, two and one-half gallons will be needed. It is best to make up at one time all the brine needed on one day. A clean tub or barrel can be used for mixing the brine. Pour the brine over the vegetables and cover. Set the vessel and its contents away in a moderately warm room to ferment.

When fermentation ceases, the container should be placed in a cool cellar or storeroom and the surface of the liquid treated to prevent mold. Before adding the paraffin or cottonseed oil, any scum or mold which may have formed on the surface of the liquid should be removed by skimming.

These general directions can always be followed with successful results, but some modifications are desirable for certain vegetables.

Cucumbers—Dill Style. To pickle cucumbers wash the cucumbers and pack into a clean, water-tight barrel, keg or crock. On the bottom of the barrel place a layer of dill weed and a handful of mixed spice. Add another layer of dill and another handful of spice when the barrel is half full, and when almost full, add a third layer. If a keg or crock is used, the amount of dill and spice can be reduced in proportion to the size of the receptacle. When the container has been filled to within a few inches of the top, add a layer of covering material— beet leaves or grape leaves—about an inch thick. If any spoilage should occur on the surface, this layer will protect the vegetables beneath. Press down with a clean board weighted with bricks or stone.

Make the brine as given in the general rules. Add sufficient brine to cover the material and allow it to stand twenty-four hours. Then make air-tight. The time necessary for complete fermentation to occur depends upon the temperature. In a warm place five days to a week may suffice; in a cool cellar three to four weeks.

The dill and spices may be omitted, in which case we then have plain cucumbers.

String Beans. Remove the ends and strings from the beans and cut into pieces about two inches long; pack in the container; cover with brine and ferment.

Green Tomatoes. Green tomatoes should be packed whole and prepared as cucumbers. The dill and spice may be added if desired.

Beets. Beets must be scrubbed thoroughly and packed whole. If peeled or sliced before being fermented the beets lose considerable color and flavor.

Beet Tops and Turnip Tops. These should be washed thoroughly and packed into the container without being cut up.

Peas. Green peas should be shelled and packed in the same way as string beans. It is advisable to use fairly small containers for peas, so that the quantity opened up will be used before it has a chance to spoil.

Corn. Husk and clean the silk from the corn; wash and place the ears on end in the jar, packing the jar nearly full. Pour the brine over the ears; add cover and weights. Fermented corn has a sour taste, which may not be relished if the corn is eaten alone. For this reason it will be preferable in most cases to preserve corn by canning, drying or by salting without fermentation. Fermented corn, however, may be used in the preparation of some dishes, such as chowders, omelets, and so forth, where its flavor will be masked to some extent by the other ingredients. To some people this peculiar acid taste of fermented corn is not at all objectionable.

Salting Without Fermentation. In this method the vegetables are packed with enough salt to prevent fermentation or the growth of yeasts or molds. The vegetables preserved most satisfactorily by this method are dandelions, beet tops, turnip tops, spinach, kale, chard, cabbage, cauliflower, string beans, green peas and corn. The following directions should be followed:

The vegetables should be washed, drained and weighed. The amount of salt needed will be a quarter of the weight of the vegetables. Kegs or crocks make satisfactory containers. Put a layer of vegetables about an inch thick on the bottom of the container. Cover this with salt. Continue making alternate layers of vegetables and salt until the container is almost filled. The salt should be evenly distributed so that it will not be necessary to use more salt than the quantity required in proportion to the weights of the vegetables that are used.

Cover the surface with a cloth, and a board of glazed plate. Place a weight on these and set aside in a cool place. If sufficient liquor to cover the vegetables has not been extracted pour in enough strong brine—one pound of salt to two quarts of water—to cover the surface round the corner.

The top layer of vegetables should be kept under the brine to prevent molding. There will be some bubbling at first. As soon as this stops, set the container where it will not be disturbed until ready for use. Seal by pouring very hot paraffin over the surface.

String beans should be cut in two-inch pieces. Peas should be shelled. Cabbage should be shredded in the same way as for sauerkraut. Corn, however, requires somewhat different treatment, and the directions for salting it are as follows:

Salted Corn. Husk the ears of corn and remove the silk. Cook in boiling water for about ten minutes to set the milk. Cut off the corn from the cob with a sharp knife. Weigh the corn and pack in layers with a quarter its weight of fine salt, as described above.

Some experts insist on blanching and cold-dipping all vegetables for dry-salting without fermentation. They say that, though it is not necessary, it makes the tissues softer and consequently they are more easily penetrated by the salt. Furthermore, when preparing these products for the table the salt soaks out more readily and the products cook much more quickly if they have been blanched. So where there is time it seems advisable to blanch for five minutes for dry-salting.

If properly prepared and stored, fermented, brined and dry-salted products will keep for a long time. It is absolutely necessary to prevent mold from growing on the surface of the brine of fermented vegetables, by the addition of paraffin or in some other way. Protection of the surface of dry-salted vegetables is desirable, but not necessary if the containers are covered to prevent the evaporation of the brine. Most trouble with the fermented or salted products may be traced to carelessness in protecting the surface of the brine.

POINTS TO REMEMBER

These are the special things to remember about fermentation, brining and dry-salting:

1. For fermentation, such as in making sauerkraut, use a quarter pound of salt to ten pounds of food material. For every 100 pounds of food add two and a half pounds of salt.

2. For brining use three-quarters of a cupful of salt and one cupful of vinegar to each gallon of water.

3. For dry-salting use one pound of salt to four pounds of food.

4. Do not use vinegar, pickle or pork barrels as containers for salted foods unless they are very thoroughly scalded.

5. Thoroughly scald all containers, covers, weights and cloths before using.

6. If using glass jars put a cork inside to press the food down. If white vaseline is rubbed on the rubber rings the solution will not get through rubber and be lost.

7. After adding salt or brine for fermented foods, cover the food material with a piece of muslin or cheesecloth six inches larger in diameter than the diameter of the container. Tuck this in round the top of the food, cover with weight and adjust lid of container.

8. During fermentation keep the cover on loosely until all bubbles cease. Test by slightly knocking container to see if any bubbles appear on the surface.

9. When you have made this test and discovered that the bubbling has ceased, then it is time to protect the food from all organisms which destroy lactic acid.

10. To protect the food cover with hot melted paraffin or liquid oil.

11. If evaporation takes place, add water or brine to make up the original amount of water.

12. When dry sealing is used let the product stand twenty-four to thirty-six hours, then add strong brine to fill the containers. The water from the vegetables usually only half fills the containers.

TABLE FOR PRESERVATION OF VEGETABLES BY SALT

METHODS VEGETABLES ADAPTED TO METHOD AMOUNT OF SALT OTHER INGREDIENTS NEEDED I. Dry salting with fermentation. Cabbage, which is converted by this method into sauerkraut, string beans, beet tops, turnip tops, greens, kale and dandelions. ¼-lb. salt to 10 lbs. food or 2½ lbs. salt to 100 lbs. food. No other. II. Fermentation with brine. Cucumbers, string beans, green tomatoes, beets, beet tops, corn and green peas. ¾-cup salt, 1 gallon water, 1 cup vinegar for brine. Amount of brine required is equal to ½ volume of food. Dill and spices can be added. 1 lb. dry dill or 2 lbs. green dill and 1 oz. spices for a>4-gallon crock. III. Dry salting without fermentation. Dandelions, beet tops, turnip tops, spinach, kale, chard, cabbage, cauliflower, string beans, green peas, and corn. 25 lbs. salt to 100 lbs. of food. Salt should be ¼ weight of vegetable. Blanch and cold-dip vegetables for five minutes before dry salting.

CHAPTER XVI

CURING, SMOKING AND PRESERVING MEAT

Many farmers seem to have more trouble with the curing of meats than with the slaughtering. This part of the work is indeed very important as it determines whether one will have good tasting cured meat or meat that is too salty or possibly that is far removed from the original taste of the raw product.

It is worth every farmer or farmerette's

attention to spend some time on this problem as it
pays so well in the resulting, good tasting meat.
Why not have a superior grade of home-cured meat
as easily as a poor grade? Work carefully and
accurately done will produce good results while
work slovenly or carelessly done can produce
nothing but poor results. To cure meat so that it is
not only delicious but has good keeping qualities is
an art and accomplishment worth striving for. A
pride in this work is just as fine and worth while as
the housewife's pride in her culinary skill or the
pride of any other professional in his or her line of
work. To-day we are thinking of food and its
problems as never before and it behooves us all to
put more time, thought, care and skill on all things
that pertain to foods. And as meat is such an
essential item in our diet, meat problems should
receive their due attention.

All meat that is to be cured should always be
thoroughly cooled and cut into the desired
convenient sizes before it is put into the brine or
packed in dry salt.

The pieces most commonly used for curing
are the ham, shoulder and bacon pieces from pork.
From beef we use the cheaper, tougher cuts such as
the plate, shoulder and chuck ribs. Mutton is seldom
cured and preserved.

The ham should be cut off at the hock joint,
the spare ribs taken out of the bacon, and the ragged
edges trimmed off smooth. If ragged edges or
scraggy ends are left these portions will become too
dry in the curing and will practically be wasted.

After all the animal heat is removed from
the meat and it is properly cut it is then ready for
the curing. If salt is put on the meat before the

animal heat is all removed, it will have a tendency to shrink the muscles and form a coating on the outside which will not allow the generating gases to escape. Meat should never be in a frozen condition when the salt is added as the frost will prevent the proper penetration of the brine and uneven curing will be the result.

METHODS OF CURING MEAT

The two most common methods of curing meat are first the brine or sugar cure process and second the dry-curing process. For general farm use the brine cured process is the better. It requires less time, less effort and not such an exacting place for the work. On most farms it is impossible to secure a desirable place in which to do the dry-curing as the meat is exposed to rats, cats, flies and other insects. The dry-curing requires considerable time to rub and salt the meat at different times while the only attention that is necessary for brine-curing is to properly prepare and pack the meat in the vessel and prepare the brine for it.

UTENSILS FOR CURING

If possible use a round container for the curing. It is easier to put the meat in tightly, and the space can be used to better advantage. A hardwood barrel of some kind is excellent. Sirup, molasses or lard barrels which have been thoroughly cleaned are very satisfactory. If you use a vinegar or an oil barrel it should be well burned on the inside before using. Stone crocks or jars are sometimes used but they are expensive and cumbersome to handle besides the constant danger of loss of brine from breakage.

PRESERVATIVES

For curing the meat the farmer usually uses salt, salt peter, white or brown sugar or molasses. These are the necessary preservatives. The others such as boracic acid, borax and soda are often used for sweetening the brine and to keep it from spoiling but are not absolutely essential. The salt extracts moisture and acts as a preservative. The sugar or molasses imparts a nice flavor and has a tendency to keep the muscle tissue soft in contrast to the salt, which has a tendency to make it hard and dry. So the salt and sugar have two distinct functions to perform, the one to harden and preserve, the other to soften and sweeten. If you have a favorite recipe that has proved satisfactory and you want to use sorghum or molasses instead of sugar add one pound more of the molasses. If you have been accustomed to using 2 pounds of sugar then use 3 pounds of the other sweetening.

Salt peter is not absolutely necessary as far as the preserving is concerned but it helps to hold the red color of the lean meat. If salt peter is not used the lean meat will be gray in color. It may possibly be a little tenderer if the salt peter is not used as the salt peter tends to harden the meat. Chili salt peter can be substituted in place of salt peter, if only four-fifths as much is used.

THE SUGAR BRINE CURE

All formulas for the sugar brine cure are practically the same varying only a little in the proportions of sugar, salt and salt peter. If you have a formula that you have tried for years and have found it to be satisfactory there is no reason you should attempt a new one. But for those who want to try a different formula or recipe I will give you this reliable one that is widely used and indorsed by several agricultural colleges.

The container should be scalded thoroughly. Sprinkle a layer of salt over the bottom and over each layer of meat as it is packed in, skin down. When full, cover meat with boards and weight down with a stone so that all will be below the brine, which is made as follows:

Weigh out for each 100 pounds of meat, 8 pounds of salt, 2 pounds of sugar (preferably brown) or 3 pounds of molasses, and 2 ounces of salt peter. Dissolve all in 4 gallons of water. This should be boiled, and when thoroughly cooled, cover the meat. Seven days after brine is put on, meat should be repacked in another barrel in reverse order. The pieces that were on top should be placed on the bottom. The brine is poured over as before. This is repeated on the fourteenth and twenty-first days, thus giving an even cure to all pieces. Bacon should remain in the brine from four to six weeks, and hams six to eight weeks, depending on the size of the pieces. When cured, each piece should be scrubbed with tepid water and hung to drain several days before smoking; no two pieces should come in contact. For all curing always use dairy salt and *not table* salt, as the latter contains starch to keep it dry and this starch may cause the meat to spoil. If you carefully follow these directions you will have delicious sugar-cured hams and bacon.

CORNED BEEF

It is desirable to have an ample supply of corned beef on hand. For this any part of the beef may be used but the parts usually selected are the plate, rump, cross-ribs and brisket, which are the tougher cuts of the meat. The brisket and plate are especially good because of the character of the fat, which is somewhat like a tissue. Cut all around the meat to about the same thickness, so that it will make an even layer in the barrel. It is best to remove the bone, although this is not necessary. Be sure to start the pickling or curing while the meat is perfectly fresh, but well chilled. Do not wait like some farmers do until they think the meat is beginning to spoil and then salt it down just to save it. Allow ten pounds of dairy salt to each 100 pounds of meat. Sprinkle a layer of the salt in the bottom of the crock, barrel, or whatever container is used. Have the salt about one-fourth of an inch in depth. After the layer is in the bottom of the container put the cuts of meat in as closely as possible, making the layer five or six inches in thickness, then put on another layer of salt, following that with another layer of meat. Repeat until the meat and salt have all been packed in the barrel, care being taken to reserve salt enough for a good layer on the top. Cover the meat with a board and weight down with a stone and *not* an *iron* weight. Do not allow any meat to project from the salt or mold will start and the brine will spoil in a short time. Let the meat stand over-night.

Prepare a brine by boiling 7 pounds salt, 3 pounds brown sugar or 6 pounds molasses, 2 ounces baking soda, 2 ounces salt peter and 4 gallons water for every 100 pounds of meat. This quantity of brine should be sufficient to cover that amount.

Remove any scum that rises to the surface and filter the hot brine through muslin. Set the brine aside, best over-night, to become perfectly cold before using. In the morning tip the container in which the meat is packed so that all liquor which has separated from the meat over night may drain off. Cover the meat with the cold brine. Put the container in a cool place. The curing will be more satisfactory if the meat is left at a temperature of about 38 degrees F. Never let the temperature go above 50 degrees F. and there is some risk with even a temperature of 40 degrees F. if it is continuous. The sugar or molasses in the brine has a tendency to ferment in a warm place.

After about five days the meat should be overhauled and repacked, putting the pieces which were previously on the bottom on top. Pour back the same brine, and five days later repeat the overhauling. This may seem like some trouble and possibly look like a useless waste of time but it is well worth while as it insures a more rapid and uniform curing of the meat.

When unpacking the meat watch the brine to see that it is not ropy or moldy. If you find either condition existing remove the meat and rinse each piece with cold water and after scalding the container pack the meat as at first with a little salt. Scald and skim the brine and after it is cold pour it on the meat as before. You can use corned beef if necessary after a week in the cure, but it is not thoroughly cured until it has been from 20 to 30 days in the brine. If kept for sixty days it will be salty enough to need freshening before cooking.

If the meat has been corned during the winter, and is to be kept until summer, watch the brine closely during the spring as it is more likely to spoil then than at any other time.

PLAIN SALT PORK

Rub each piece of meat with dairy salt, and pack closely in a container. Let stand over-night. The next day weigh out ten pounds of salt and two ounces of salt peter for each 100 pounds of meat, and dissolve in four gallons of boiling water. Pour this brine, when cold, over the meat, cover, and weight the meat down to keep it under the brine. The pork should be kept in the brine until used.

SMOKING CURED MEATS

Of course many farmers never attempt to smoke their cured meats but use them directly from the brine but if possible it is more satisfactory to smoke them before using for several reasons. First, the process of smoking helps to preserve the meat. The creosote formed by the combustion of the wood closes the pores of the meat to a great extent thus excluding the air and helping it to keep and at the same time makes the meat objectionable to insects. In the second place, pickled or cured meats taste better and are more palatable if smoked. Of course the smoking must be properly done and the right kind of fuel must be used.

The Smokehouse and the Smoke. It is not necessary to have a regular smokehouse—although it is a delightful addition to any farm. Here again a community meat ring is of great advantage. One smokehouse will answer for many families. This is the ideal arrangement and it can easily be managed if you are progressive and anxious enough to supply your family with delicious meat the year around saving time and money.

If, however, you have to do your own smoking and smoke only a small quantity at a time a barrel or box will answer. Overheating of the meat must be guarded against.

Green hickory or any of the hardwoods or maple should be used for the smoking. Pine or any other resinous woods should not be used as they give a disagreeable flavor to the meat. If it is impossible to get hardwood use corncobs rather than soft wood. The corncobs will leave a dirty deposit on the meat, which is carbon. It is not objectionable only from the standpoint of "looks." The meat which you are going to smoke should be removed from the brine the day before the smoking. A half hour soaking in cold water prevents a crust of salt from forming on the outside. Do not hang the meat so that any two pieces touch as this would prevent uniform smoking.

Always start with a slow fire so as to warm the meat up gradually. Thirty-six to forty-eight hours of heat as near 120 degrees F. as possible will be sufficient under most circumstances.

How to Store Smoked Meats. A dry, cool

cellar or attic where there is good circulation is a good place for storage. If the meat is to be used soon the meat can hang without coverings but for long keeping you will have to wrap it when cold in waxed paper and then in burlap, muslin or canvas bags and then hang it, after it is tied very tightly to prevent insects from getting in, in a room with a cool uniform temperature.

Some farmers get satisfactory results by wrapping the meats in strong bags and then burying them in oat bins.

SAUSAGE

Frequently when animals are butchered on the farm there are often wholesome portions of the carcass that are not used. All trimmings, cheeks, liver, tongue, breast and other pieces can be made into bologna, headcheese or some other form of sausage. Sausage making is an art worth acquiring. There is always a good demand for fresh and smoked country sausage, so if you wish to sell some you will have no trouble in finding a market for your product if it is a good one.

To make sausage you should have a meat grinder, which is an absolute essential on every farm. If you do not have one already then buy a No. 22 or No. 32.

In addition to the grinder you will need a stuffer attachment which costs very little. A knife, cord, string, a clean tube and casings or muslin bags will complete your equipment. The muslin bags can be of any size but the easiest to handle are 12 inches long and 2 inches in diameter. If the sausage is stuffed into these bags they must be paraffined for home use. If you do not want to bother with casings or bags put the sausage in stone crocks or tin pans with a layer of lard or paraffin on top.

The best sausage is made by using 3 parts of lean meat to one of fat. When using the grinder, distribute the lean and fat meat as uniformly as possible.

You are not necessarily limited to pork sausage, for there are many other delicious varieties you can make. They vary in the different kinds of meat used and in the different seasonings and spices.

Breakfast sausage has bread added to it; frankfurters are smoked pork sausage in casings; liver sausage has pork and beef or veal and bread in it; and blood sausage, as its name suggests, has blood (preferably from a hog) added to it. Then there is tomato sausage which is made of pulp from fresh tomatoes, pork sausage and crackers. Summer sausage is made in the winter and kept for use during the summer. After being dried and cured it will keep for months. Brain sausage is delicious. To make it calves' brains are mixed with lean pork. Cambridge sausage has rice added to it.

Headcheese is usually made from the hog's head but odds and ends also can be used not only from pork but from beef and veal.

Scrapple usually means the head and feet of hogs but it can be made from any hog meat. It is a good food as it uses cornmeal. It makes a change from fried mush and most men working on a farm relish it.

Sausage can be made from mutton mixed with pork in much the same way as beef is used for

similar purposes. A general formula would be 2
parts of mutton to 3 parts pork with seasonings.

With a plentiful supply of good home-cured
and home-smoked meats, together with several
varieties of sausages, you can feel you are well
equipped to feed your family with its share of meat.
Everything will have been utilized, nothing will
have been wasted. You produced your own meat,
you slaughtered and cured and smoked it and put all
trimmings and other "left-overs" into appetizing
food for your family and you have saved money.
You have utilized things at hand and required no
transportation facilities. And best of all, you have
the very finest in the land for your family and that
gives one a perfectly justifiable pride in the work
accomplished.

CHAPTER XVII

PRESERVED OR "CANNED" EGGS

As one-half of the yearly egg crop is
produced in March, April, May and June consumers
would do well to store enough at that time to use
when production is light. Fifty dozen eggs should
be stored for a family of five to use during the
months of October, November, December and
January, at which time the market price of eggs is at
the highest.

When canning them *the eggs must be fresh*, preferably not more than two or three days old. This is the reason why it is much more satisfactory to put away eggs produced in one's own chicken yard or one's neighbor's.

Infertile eggs are best if they can be obtained—so, after the hatching exclude the roosters from the flock and kill them for table use as needed.

The shells must be clean. Washing an egg with a soiled shell lessens its keeping quality. The protective gelatinous covering over the shell is removed by water and when this is gone the egg spoils more rapidly. Use the soiled eggs for immediate use and the clean ones for storage.

The shells also must be free from even the tiniest crack. One cracked egg will spoil a large number of sound eggs when packed in water glass.

Earthenware crocks are good containers. *The crocks must be clean and sound.* Scald them and let them cool completely before use. A crock holding six gallons will accommodate eighteen dozen eggs and about twenty-two pints of solution. Too large crocks are not desirable, since they increase the liability of breaking some of the eggs, and spoiling the entire batch.

It must be remembered that the eggs on the bottom crack first and that those in the bottom of the crock are the last to be removed for use. Eggs can be put up in smaller crocks and the eggs put in the crock first should be used first in the household.

METHOD OF STORING
There are many satisfactory methods of

storing eggs. The commercial method is that of cold storage and if it were not for this method winter eggs would be beyond the average purse.

The fact that eggs have been held in cold storage does not necessarily mean that they are of low quality. Carefully handled cold-storage eggs often are of better quality than fresh local eggs that have been improperly cared for.

In the home they may be packed by several methods: Salt, oats or bran; covering them with vaseline, butter, lard, paraffin or prepared ointments; immersion in brine, salicylic acid, water glass (sodium silicate) or limewater.

Any of these methods will keep the eggs for short periods if stored in a cool place. The salt, oats and bran are very satisfactory. The ointments also are satisfactory. The water glass and limewater will keep eggs without loss for a year. However, it is not wise to put down more eggs than is necessary to tide over the period of high price.

WATER GLASS METHOD

"Water glass" is known to the chemist as sodium silicate. It can be purchased by the quart from druggists or poultry supply men. It is a pale yellow, odorless, sirupy liquid. It is diluted in the proportion of one part of silicate to nine parts of distilled water, rain water, or other water. *In any case, the water should be boiled and then allowed to cool.* Half fill the vessel with this solution and place the eggs in it, being careful not to crack them. The eggs can be added a few at a time until the container is filled. Be sure to keep about two inches of water glass above the eggs. Cover the crock to prevent evaporation and place it in the coolest place available from which the crock will not have to be moved. Wax paper covered over and tied around the top of the crock can be used. Inspect the crock from time to time and replace any water that has evaporated with cool boiled water.

LIMEWATER METHOD

Limewater is also satisfactory for preserving eggs and is slightly less expensive than water glass. A solution is made by placing two or three pounds of unslaked lime in five gallons of water, which has been boiled and allowed to cool, and allowing the mixture to stand until the lime settles and the liquid is clear. The eggs should be placed in a clean earthenware jar or other suitable vessel and covered to a depth of two inches with the liquid. Remove the eggs as desired, rinse in clean, cold water and use immediately.

If using the limewater method add a little of the lime sediment to insure a constantly saturated solution. If a thin white crust appears on the limewater solution it is due to the formation of calcium carbonate coming in contact with the air and consequently does no harm.

CANDLING EGGS AT HOME

If you purchase the eggs that are to be stored it is safer to candle them. Examining eggs to determine their quality is called "candling." Every

one knows that some eggs are better than others, but
the ease with which the good ones can be picked
out is not generally understood. The better the
quality of eggs, the surer the housewife can be that
they will keep satisfactorily.

HOMEMADE CANDLER

The equipment for candling usually consists
of either a wooden, a metal, or a cardboard box and
a kerosene lamp or an electric light. A very
inexpensive egg candler for home use can be made
from a large shoe-box or similar cardboard box.
Remove the ends of the box, and cut a hole about
the size of a half-dollar in one side. Slip the box
over the lamp or electric bulb, darken the room,
hold the egg, with the large end up, before the
opening in the box and its quality can easily be
judged.

SIGNS OF A GOOD EGG

When held before the opening of the candle,
good eggs will look clear and firm. The air cell (the
white spot at the large end of the eggs) should be
small, not larger than a dime, and the yolk may be
dimly seen in the center of the egg. A large air cell
and a dark, freely moving yolk indicate that the egg
is stale.

If the shell contents appear black or very
dark, the egg is absolutely unfit for food. If you are
in doubt about the quality of any eggs you are
candling break a few of them into a dish and

examine them. This is an excellent way to learn to know how good and bad eggs look when they are being candled.

Discard all eggs that have shrunken, loose contents, a watery appearance, cracked and thin shells. Eggs of this description will not keep and are apt to spoil the eggs close around them. Any egg that floats in the solution should be discarded.

When packing eggs whether in salt, oats, or in solution place them with small end down. When packing them in salt, oats, etc., do not allow any two eggs to touch.

PACKING THE EGGS

One gallon of water glass as purchased will make enough preservative to preserve from 75 to 100 dozen eggs.

Three gallons of either water glass solution or limewater solution will preserve from 200 to 240 dozen eggs according to the size of the eggs and the shape of the container.

The cost of preserving eggs by the water glass method is about one cent per dozen eggs, not considering the cost of the container. The lime water method is still cheaper.

The following gives the sizes of jars with approximate capacity for eggs and the amount of water glass solution required to cover the eggs:

1 gallon jar—40 eggs, 3½ pints of solution or 1¾ qt.

2 gallon jar—80 eggs, 8 pints of solution or 2 quarts.

3 gallon jar—120 eggs, 11 pints of solution

or 5½ quarts.

    4 gallon jar—160 eggs, 14½ pints of solution or 7¼ quarts.

    5 gallon jar—200 eggs, 18 pints of solution or 9 quarts.

    6 gallon jar—216 eggs, 22 pints of solution or 11 quarts.

    10 gallon jar—400 eggs, 36 pints of solution or 18 quarts.

HOW TO USE PRESERVED EGGS

When the eggs are to be used, remove them as desired, rinse in clean, cold water, and use immediately.

Eggs preserved in water glass can be used for soft boiling or poaching up to November. Before boiling such eggs prick a tiny hole in the large end of the shell with a needle to keep them from cracking, as the preservative seals the pores of the shell and prevents the escape of gases, which is possible in the strictly fresh egg.

They are satisfactory for frying until about December. From that time until the end of the usual storage period—that is until March—they can be used for omelettes, scrambled eggs, custards, cakes and general cookery. As the eggs age, the white becomes thinner and is harder to beat. The yolk membrane becomes more delicate and it is correspondingly difficult to separate the whites from the yolks. Sometimes the white of the egg is tinged pink after very long keeping in water glass. This is due, probably, to a little iron which is in the sodium silicate, but which apparently does not injure the eggs for food purposes.

CHAPTER XVIII

HOME STORAGE OF VEGETABLES

Towards the end of the canning season most housewives have used every available glass jar and tin can and hesitate about purchasing a new supply. They have dried and brined many products and yet they feel, and rightly so, that they would like still more vegetables for winter use. There still remains another method that they may employ to provide themselves with a plentiful supply of vegetables and these vegetables can be in the fresh state too. Neither canned, dried, pickled or salted but fresh.

Canning, drying, pickling and salting are essential and necessary but they can not take the place of storage. To keep vegetables in their natural state is the easiest and simplest form of food preservation. Of course, you must take proper precautions against freezing and decay. If you do this you can have an abundant supply of many kinds of fresh vegetables all winter, where climatic and living conditions will permit. Storage costs but little money and little effort and yet it is very satisfactory.

There are many vegetables that can be stored to good advantage. They are: Beets, Brussels Sprouts, Beans, Celery, Carrots, Chicory or Endive,

Cabbage, Cauliflower, Kohl-rabi, Lima Beans,
Onions, Sweet Potatoes, Squash (Winter), Salsify or
Vegetable Oyster, Tomatoes, Turnips.

To get good results in any kind of storage,
you must observe four things:

1. Proper ventilation.
2. Proper regulation of temperature.
3. Sufficient moisture.
4. Good condition of vegetables when
stored.

There are six different ways to store
vegetables. They are: cellar storage, pit storage,
outdoor cellar or cave storage, attic storage, sand
boxes and pantry storage.

CELLAR STORAGE

We will first of all consider cellar or
basement storage. One of the most convenient
places for the storage of vegetables is a cool, well-
ventilated and reasonably dry cellar underneath the
house. This cellar must have windows or some
method of ventilation, must not be too warm and
not so cold that food will freeze. If there is proper
ventilation there can be some dampness without
injury to the vegetables. If your cellar or basement
floods easily or has water standing in it anywhere it
should not be used for vegetable storage.

If there is a furnace in the cellar or basement
a small room as far as possible from the heating
plant should be partitioned off. Do not build a room
in the middle of the cellar, for two sides of the room
should consist of outside walls.

If possible have two outside windows for

proper regulation of the temperature and for good ventilation. If you cannot have two windows have one.

A very good arrangement for constant circulation of air consists in having a stove-pipe inserted through one of the lower panes of the window to admit cold air. One of the upper panes of the window can be removed to allow for the escape of warm air. That is, of course, if the window is made of nine or twelve small panes of squares of glass. In severely cold weather this upper pane can be replaced or the opening stuffed up in some way.

If you do not have an old stove-pipe you can make a wooden flue of old boards or old discarded boxes.

Most cellars and basements are now made with concrete floors. The ideal floor for storage purposes is an earth floor. However, we can put two or three inches of sand on our concrete floors and get good results. Sprinkle the sand with water from time to time.

Put the vegetables that are to be stored in boxes, baskets, barrels or crates. Use containers that hold only two or three bushels apiece. If larger boxes or barrels are used there is always danger of heating and decay. Of course, proper precautions should be taken against mice.

An excellent way to prevent wilting of crops and shrinkage is to put moist leaves, oak or maple, in the containers with the vegetables. Moist sand is sometimes used but it is much heavier to handle than the leaves. It is no difficult matter to rake the lawn when you are ready to store the vegetables.

The vegetables that are adapted for cellar storage are beets, cabbage, carrots, celery, parsnips, potatoes, salsify and turnips.

PIT STORAGE

There are two kinds of pits that may be used for storage. Those that are not frost-proof and those which are frost-proof.

Some vegetables are not injured by being held in a frozen condition during the winter months. Cabbage is not injured by moderate frost. Cabbage and parsnips will stand freezing and a little thawing, so they can be put in pits or better still, boxes or barrels set into the ground may be used. Make the pit mound shaped. If the earth is mounded around the box, barrel or pit, surface water cannot run in.

If using this kind of storage do not store the products until both the ground and the products are frozen solid. The idea is to keep the vegetables frozen or to have very few freezings and thawings, and those few should be gradual.

After the pit has been made or the box or barrel has been set into the ground and filled with vegetables, it should be covered first with a piece of burlap or carpet, then with a mouse-proof board cover and finally with straw or similar material. When taken from the pit, the vegetables can be thawed out over night in cold water, after which they can be kept in the cellar for a short length of time.

The pits for keeping vegetables free from frost must be carefully and thoughtfully made, but they are cheap and are very useful and practical when caves or cellars are not convenient.

The frost-proof pit for storing vegetables should always be placed in as well-drained a place as possible. A shallow excavation should be made from one to two feet deep, four feet wide and as long as desired. Line the pit with straw, hay or leaves, then place the vegetables in a conical pile on the straw. Cover the vegetables with six inches of the material used in making the lining. This is covered with three or four inches of earth. The straw is allowed to extend up through the earth at the top of the pile, thus assuring ventilation.

When it becomes colder add more covering to the pit by another layer of straw and a layer of earth. In very cold climates a layer of manure or corn stalks will afford protection against frost.

It is well to make several small pits rather than one larger one for the reason that when a pit has once been opened it is difficult to protect the remaining vegetables from frost.

It is advisable to store several varieties of vegetables in one pit so that when each pit is opened you have a variety of vegetables. If you follow this plan separate the various crops by using straw or leaves.

Pits are entered by chopping a hole through the frozen earth at one end, large enough to reach into or crawl into. After the vegetables have been obtained keep the hole stuffed and covered most carefully and deeply with old sacks and straw.

If the smaller pits are used, a decidedly better arrangement, take out all the vegetables in the pit and those that are not needed for immediate consumption can be placed in the cellar storage room, or other cool place, until needed. Do not use those pits if you live where winter rains are abundant as the pits will become water soaked and the vegetables will suffer more or less decay.

OUTDOOR CELLAR STORAGE

Outdoor cellars or caves may be cheaply built for more or less temporary use or they may be very expensively built of concrete, brick, or clay blocks. Of course, the latter are permanent storing places and offer perfect storage for potatoes, carrots, cabbages, parsnips, beets, turnips and salsify.

The objectionable features of indoor cellar storage is that such storage does not furnish ideal conditions for keeping the vegetables fresh for any great length of time.

The objectionable feature to the pit storage is the inaccessibility to these pits during severe weather.

The outdoor cellar or cave overcomes both these objections. The outdoor cellar or cave is an underground structure, preferably built in a hillside and fully covered with earth except at one end only where the entrance is located. If there are doors at both ends it is almost impossible to prevent freezing in very cold weather. The cave door should fit perfectly and there should be a hatchway or door over the steps leading down to the cave door.

A very satisfactory inexpensive cellar can be made by digging an excavation about 5 ft. deep and in this erecting a frame by setting posts in rows near the dirt walls. Saw these posts off at uniform height and place plates on their tops. On these plates place rafters. Board up completely with the exception of the entrance. Cover the whole with dirt or sod and in cold climates add a layer of straw or fodder.

A ventilation must be provided in the roof at the back end. A sewer tile with the bell end up makes a very good flue. A dirt floor is satisfactory as it contains moisture. If there is any seepage use a drain tile to carry it off.

The more pretentious permanent cellars are provided with air spaces to furnish insulation; are provided with large ventilation shafts through the roof and cold air intakes under the floor. Thorough drainage is obtained by placing a line of tile around the outside wall and also by having the air intake serve as a drain for surplus water that might get into the cave. The floor is cement or concrete. Such a cave is expensive but is a permanent structure and a good addition to any farm or estate. If properly made it is possible to maintain a temperature of 34 to 38 degrees without much fluctuation during the winter months. This kind of storage is not only adapted for vegetables but apples as well. It is better adapted to the Northern, Eastern and Western States than to the Southern States, where it is likely to be warm at the time the vegetables are ready for storage. When making the cave, have it as near as possible to the kitchen door. Sometimes caves are made so that they can be entered from the house, cellar or porch.

ATTIC STORAGE

Some vegetables such as onions, squashes, sweet potatoes and pumpkins can be stored in the attic in crates which allow free circulation of air. They must be absolutely free from bruises and must be well ripened and cured. To cure the vegetables expose them to the air for a few days in the shade. Remove the tops of onions before storing. The attic is much better for storing onions than the basement.

Squashes are susceptible to cold and moisture, so are suitable for the attic.

Be very careful in handling the squashes to prevent breaking the stems off. Watch pumpkins and squash carefully and at the first sign of decay, use immediately or can.

SAND BOX STORAGE

Sand boxes in cellars, pits or caves are desirable for beets, turnips, kohl-rabi, carrots, winter radishes and rutabagas. The sand keeps them cold and prevents evaporation. Kohl-rabi should be tender when stored.

PANTRY STORAGE

Where there is no attic or where it is inconveniently reached, the products that are adapted to a very dry place can be stored on the pantry shelves or in a dry cellar near the furnace. They are onions, squashes, pumpkins and sweet potatoes.

The keeping qualities of all these vegetables, no matter what storage is used, depends chiefly upon their condition when placed in storage. All products to be stored must be mature, but not overgrown. Root crops should be dry while the ground is in good working condition. All vegetables should be allowed to become surface dry before placing them in storage.

White or Irish potatoes, especially, should not be exposed to bright sunlight any length of time.

Only vegetables free from disease or injury should
be stored. Any that are damaged can be used
immediately, or can be canned or dried.

Further particulars for the storing of fresh
vegetables are given in the following tables.

TABLE FOR VEGETABLE STORAGE
VEGETABLES HOW BEST STORED
PREPARATION FOR STORAGE AMOUNT FOR
FAMILY OF TWO REMARKS Irish Potatoes Must
be kept cool with a slight degrees of moisture. Use
either cellar or cave methods. No potato should be
more than four ft. from air if stored in barrels,
boxes, crates or bins. Potatoes must be dug before
the ground is crusted with frost. Frosted potatoes
will spoil, one after another. Impossible to sort out
frosted potatoes. 10 to 15 bus. Remember Irish
potatoes are ruined by freezing. Potatoes should be
kept absolutely dark to prevent greening by light.
Never buy potatoes in sacks that show wet places
due to a frosted potato. Sweet Potatoes Require
warmth and dryness. In crates or on shelves in
warm dry room. Can be spread on the floor in the
room above the kitchen where they will have plenty
of heat, especially for the first 2 or 3 weeks after
they are dug. When the sweet potatoes are dug they
should be allowed to lie in the sun and wind for 3 or
4 hours so as to become perfectly dry. They must be
well ripened and free from bruises. Can be kept on
shelves in a very dry place and they need not be
kept specially cold. Sweet potatoes keep best when
they are showing just a little inclination to sprout.
However, if they start growing the quality is greatly
injured. 2 to 3 bus. If you are in doubt as to whether
the sweet potatoes are matured enough for storage,

cut or break one end and expose it to the air for a few minutes. If the surface of the cut or break dries, the potato is mature. But if moisture remains on the surface, it is not fully ripened. In places where there are early frosts, sweet potatoes should be dug about the time the first frost is expected, without considering maturity. Carrots Are best stored in sand in cellars, caves or pits; or in tightly covered boxes or crocks. Must be kept cold and evaporation must be prevented, for otherwise they become wilted. Can remain in the ground until the weather is quite cool; then be pulled, the tops cut off and then stored. 1 to 3 bus. If you store carrots in the cellar and it is extremely dry cover them with a little moistened sand. Celery May be rooted in earth in a cellar or cave and if watered occasionally will keep fresh until Christmas. The soil, earth or sand, in which the celery is set should be 2 or 3 inches deep. This soil must not be allowed to become dry. Can remain in the ground until the weather is quite cool. 5 dozen good plants or bunches. Another way to store celery is to bank it to the top with earth; cover the tops with boards, straw, or leaves and allow it to remain where it has grown until wanted for use. Another way is to dig a trench 12 inches wide and deep enough to correspond with the height of the celery, then lift the celery and pack it in this trench with some soil about the roots. When the weather becomes colder, cover the trench with boards nailed together in the form of a V shaped trough and over this inverted trough put a layer of soil. The ends of this trough should be left open for ventilation until freezing sets in, then close these openings with straw, old bags or soil. If the freeze ceases and there is a spell of warmer weather open the ends slightly for ventilation. When the celery is first stored in the trenches the soil about the roots of the celery should be watered and and if the weather is dry after the celery is put in the trenches, pour some water around the roots to keep the celery crisp and fresh. Cabbage Can be wrapped in paper with the outer leaves left on for immediate use and stored in ventilated barrels or large crates in the cellar. But as few cellars are cool enough to keep cabbage in good condition it is more advisable to store it in a long shallow pit in the garden. Is not injured by moderate frost while in the pit but should not be disturbed while frozen. The pit should be long and narrow. Pull the cabbage, stem, root and all, and then laid with heads down about 3 heads in width can be placed in the pit. Cover lightly with soil and as the weather becomes colder add a little more soil until there is a layer 6 or 7 inches thick over the cabbage. Keep the ends of the pit partially open for ventilation until the weather becomes very cold. 25 heads. Late varieties of cabbage are the only ones fit for storage. It is advisable to dig a shallow ditch around the pit so that all surplus water can be carried off. Chickory or Endive Store in a box or bed of moist sand in the cellar. Put roots in an upright position with the sand coming just to their tops. Water the sand occasionally. Sometimes a covering of straw is added to blanch the tender growth of shoots, which is the part used as food. Late in the fall lift the roots out and carefully trim off the leaves without injury to the heart. 5 doz. roots. Chickory or endive is grown the same as carrots or salsify. It is useful in the winter for it furnishes the needed green that is so scarce in winter. Beets Must not be placed in too large piles in the cellar as they are inclined to mold. Can also be buried in pits in open ground. Can remain in the ground until very cool weather; then should be pulled, the tops cut off and then stored in the cellar. 1 bushel. Beets are not so much inclined to shrivel as carrots. Salsify or Vegetable Oyster Pack roots in box with moist sand in cellar or as they are not injured by remaining in the ground all winter they can be left there. Enough for immediate use may be dug in the autumn and the others dug as desired. When stored in the cellar after the salsify is pulled, trim off the tops and then stand them in an upright position with the sand even with the tops. 75 to 100 roots. Is injured by too much freezing and thawing, so should remain frozen. Parsnips Can be stored just as salsify or be allowed to remain in the ground until wanted. Those that are to be stored in the cellar can remain in in the garden until the weather is quite cool, then prepare and store like salsify. 1 bushel in the cellar and one in the garden. Parsnips are best kept frozen or fresh in the cellar as too much freezing and thawing destroys them. Turnips Must be stored where temperature is low or sprouting will result. Moderate freezing does no harm while in the storage pit but they must not be disturbed while frozen. Pull; cut tops off and store in sand in cellars or caves, or in pits, or in tightly covered boxes or crocks. 1 to 3 bus. The object is to keep them cold and prevent evaporation. It is a good plan to store a portion in the cellar so as to be available during the time that those buried in the pit are "frozen in" and not so easily accessible. Onions Require a cool dry place. Attic excellent. Before storing, cure them by exposing to the air for a few days in the shade. Dryness is absolutely essential. A well cured onion should be firm and not readily dented at the base of the tops by the tip of the thumb when held in the hand. 3 bushels. Onions are best for storage if topped about 1½ inches long. Cauliflower Planted in shallow boxes of soil in light place in the cellar. Must not be too mature. Store as many as possible. If kept well watered they will mature for winter use. Brussels Sprouts Planted in soil in cellar. Must not be too mature. According to family tastes. Keep watered and will mature. Ground Cherries or Husk Tomatoes Kohl-rabi, Winter Radishes, Rutabagas May be stored for some weeks in the husk in their layers in a dry place free from frost. Best stored in sand in cellars, cares or pits. Must be kept cold to prevent evaporation. According to the family tastes. Kohl-rabi must be tender when stored. Horse-radish Pumpkins May be kept in the ground where grown all winter. Must be kept frozen as thawing injures it. Best kept on shelves in a very dry place. Can be kept on shelves in furnace room. Must be ripened and cured and free from bruises. 5 ordinary sized pumpkins. Need not be kept especially cold. Squashes Susceptible to cold and moisture, so store in a dry place where temperature will be between 50 and 60 degrees. Care must be taken that stem is not broken. 10 ordinary sized hubbard squashes. Whenever squashes or pumpkins in storage show signs of decay, the sound portion should be immediately canned. Tomatoes Cool cellar or cave; can be wrapped in any absorbent paper preferably without printing upon it, and laid upon shelves to ripen. The paper absorbs the moisture given off by the tomatoes and causes them to ripen uniformly. If cellar is dry or well ventilated, tomatoes can be kept a month or six weeks in this manner. May be kept until Christmas if vines with the green tomatoes hanging on them are pulled and hung in the cellar. Pull the vines before they are frosted. All that you can put away. Most of the tomatoes that are put into storage will ripen and be most acceptable as soon as they color up. If these tomatoes, when cooked, are found to be very acid, the acidity may be overcome by using baking soda. Parsley Transplant into flower pots late in the fall. Keep in windows where they will receive plenty of sunshine.   Garlic Should be thoroughly cured as are onions. Or it may be braided by the tops into strings which are hung up in dry places for curing and storing.   Head Lettuce Rooted in earth in a cellar or cave. Water occasionally. All you have in the garden.   Dry beans and peas Stored where protected from weevils. Should be fully ripened before shelling. Pick pods by hand as they ripen and spread pods to become thoroughly dry. May be shelled by spreading pods on a sheet and beating them with a stick. Can be cleaned by pouring them from a height of 4 or 5 ft. upon a sheet and allowing the wind to blow the particles of pod out of them as they fall. As many as you can gather.   Apples Must be kept in a dry, cool place and so stored as to be in no danger of absorbing odors from vegetables stored nearby. Apples absorb odors from potatoes, onions, turnips and other strong vegetables. Sort apples carefully removing and using at once all fruit that is bruised and shows signs of decay. The best results are obtained by wrapping each apple in half a sheet of newspaper and storing in barrels, boxes, crates or bins. The wrapping prevents apples from touching and thus prevents decay. It also protects apples from

odors of vegetables stored nearby. As many barrels
of apples as possible. Remember that "An apple a
day will keep the doctor away." The cellar or other
storage place must be kept cool. 32° F. is ideal.
Never allow temperature to go above 40° F. They
can be stored unwrapped in barrels, boxes, crates,
bins, etc., if proper attention is paid to sorting, to
providing a cool place for storage, to occasional
sorting during the winter and for the immediate
removal of all decayed fruit. Even if you do not
raise apples, but have a good storage place, meeting
the requirements as regards temperature, you will
find it advantageous to buy a winter's supply in the
autumn, when prices are low.

CHAPTER XIX

HOW TO MARKET HOME CANNED
PRODUCE

You have some delicious jellies, jams,
canned fruits and vegetables that you wish to sell
and you do not know just how to go about it. There
are at your disposal several means of selling:
  1. Through advertising.
  2. Through personal letters to desirable
shops, delicatessens, boarding-houses, colleges, etc.
  3. By direct salesmanship; that is, by making
personal visits to the buyers, either homes or stores.
  4. Through jobbers to whom you pay a

commission on all sales.

5. Through coöperative selling.

Perhaps the cheapest and easiest way for you to handle your problem is to employ the method so much used to-day and that is wayside advertising. Wayside advertising costs practically nothing and yet it pays.

Autos are everywhere these days. You cannot take a country ride without seeing many signboards at the farm entrances advertising chickens, fresh eggs, vegetables, honey, apples and canned goods. I have a friend who drives 50 miles every fall for her honey. She first found it by seeing the sign in front of the farm and now she returns year after year because she thinks no other honey is just like it. She would never have discovered it if that farm woman had not been clever enough to think of advertising her goods in this cheap way. My friend told all her other "auto" friends, so the country woman has a splendid outlet for her product now. If you live on a good road that is patronized at all by autoists you ought to get your signboard up at once.

We often pass a farm where the sign "Fresh Home-Made Candy" always tempts us to stop and buy. What autoist could resist that sign? And here miles from town this clever woman is carrying on a profitable side trade, which is netting her a nice little yearly income. Her candy is good; we go often and so do many others. She has turned her profession into a paying proposition. She could send her candy away by parcel post or by some other means, but she would not be so far ahead as she is now.

In addition to your wayside advertising you

could advertise in papers, magazines, etc. Many producers believe strongly in advertising in daily and weekly papers. You can quickly find out whether this kind of advertising pays. Give it a trial at least. After you have spent ten or fifteen dollars in advertising you ought to know whether it pays.

Use one or two of the city papers near you, taking the publisher's advice as to the best day of the week on which to run the advertisement, the size and the position of the "ad." The first cost of getting your customers may seem high, but with good products you could soon build up a list of people to whom sales can be made year after year.

This form of advertising has many advantages. If your advertising copy is clever and you have some novelty to offer, you ought to receive many orders. If orders come, you get the full retail price, the shipping charges are paid by the customer, and cash comes with every order. And it means, if your customers are pleased, that you have permanent customers. The initial cost is great and there is a risk, but remember "it pays to advertise."

There are millions of city women who never can a jar of fruit or put up a single glass of preserves or jelly who will be glad to have you send your goods direct to them by parcel post. But you must get in touch with these women either through wayside advertising, magazine and paper advertising or by direct salesmanship, although very few women have the time for personal calls.

Considerable business can be done by letter writing to stores, restaurants and boarding-houses in distant cities. It may be impossible for you to go personally, in which case letters often bring the desired results. Make your letters business-like and typewrite them. Do not be discouraged if you do not get many replies at first as there are at least fifty per cent who pay no attention to such letters. But this form of advertising usually pays.

Another method followed by many home canners is that of marketing direct to the retail grocers, care being taken, of course, to protect these grocers by not selling to more than one member in a community. One of the great advantages, of this direct salesmanship is that little selling effort is required on your part after the first arrangements have been made. The nearby market plan is greatly to be recommended because you can keep in touch with your selling concern, build up a line of desirable goods and promote its sale by advertising.

Of course you can get more money for your goods if you have time and the opportunity to sell *direct to* the consumers. You will of necessity have to sell cheaper to the grocers because they too must make their profit. Marketing direct to the consumer has a special appeal to many people. Where time is available and the community accustomed to purchasing in this manner, this method offers great possibilities. The profits are of course higher but the results more uncertain, for it is somewhat difficult to gauge the demands of the public, and the canner must assume the risk ordinarily taken by the merchant.

It takes time and patience to develop a list of customers but if you have time in the winter to do this you will find it will pay you well. If you can get customers who are willing to pay good prices for quality, scrupulous cleanliness and the homemade flavor, you will get a larger gross return than if you sold through merchants, but if your time is valuable it would scarcely pay you to take individual orders and deliver goods.

There is still another way and that is to market your home-canned products in large lots to jobbers, but if this plan is to be pursued successfully there must be a reasonably large pack and wholesale rates. This method produces more uniform profits year by year, for after a reputation is established the home-canner would not experience great difficulty in thus disposing of her entire output by contract, providing the quality was high and the price demands not excessive.

But the greatest and best way of all to find a profitable market for your things is to coöperate with other canners in your own neighborhood and find a market for quantity as well as quality. Delicatessens, club houses, tea shops, college dormitories, restaurants and hotels, all pay good prices for fine quality. No big buyer will bother to purchase one or two dozen of this or that. He wants dozens of things. One of the very best profitable ways to sell with little trouble is through quantities. Get all the women in your community to bring together cans of fruit and preserves, etc., to some marketing place. Find out how many jars of currant jelly you have, how many cans of peas and corn, how many of cherries, etc., and then notify your buyer or prospective buyer.

Coöperative selling has been undertaken and found profitable. In some cases, especially in localities frequented by the summer boarder or the automobile tourist, sales are made direct to customers who come to the salesrooms of the organizations or to their special sales; in other cases goods are sent by parcel post and other means. The women in the community can hire or beg a room where all the women of the community can sell their products for individual profit. This room should be located on the direct automobile road in order to attract tourists and automobile parties. An annual membership fee of from 50 cents to $1 generally is required for these organizations, and a charge of from 10 to 15 per cent of the selling price usually is made to cover the cost of selling. In a few instances the managing board has been able to secure an efficient person to take charge of the enterprise for a specified percentage on the sales.

Wholesale grocery concerns are interested in big things—orders can be placed with them. Soda fountains in towns and cities are excellent customers for the freshest eggs they can get. They are encroaching more and more on the trade of the restaurants and lunch rooms. Many serve light luncheons and would be interested in good butter, preserves and jams. When you get a list of names and addresses write to several dozen places, tell what your organization has in the way of guaranteed eggs, homemade products and what kind of service you could offer in the way of regular shipments. When orders come it is an easy matter to look up at your local bank the responsibility of any customer, so there is little risk. Or cash can be insisted upon with every order, although large concerns prefer to pay after receipt of goods and bill.

Each woman in this coöperative organization must keep her goods up to a certain standard, for an inferior lot of goods sent to a large firm might ruin a reputation.

Three things govern the sale of canned products—appearances, quality and price. So many things enter into consideration of prices obtainable that it is difficult to set a standard which will be applicable to different sections. The quality of the pack, its neatness, the method of marketing and many other matters must be considered in deciding this all-important point. As a general proposition, however, if the products are uniformly high grade, prices may be obtained which are somewhat in excess of factory-made products marketed in the same manner.

Like any other new industry, the selling should be developed slowly in order to minimize the possibility of loss and to assure stable business. One should study the situation carefully both from the manufacturing and marketing standpoints. Plan the season's campaign before taking up the work, and do not let the enthusiasm of the beginner interfere with good business judgment.

The selling when rightly managed can be made a successful business or it can be turned into a liability through careless, unbusinesslike methods and insufficient or unwise planning. Properly handled it will pay well for the investment of time and money, and offer opportunity for the disposal of surplus home-canned, home-grown, homemade and home-prepared products of all kinds.

LIVING UP TO CONTRACTS

Care must be taken not to contract for more than can be delivered. This would be bad business, and business principles must govern in selling home products just as in other enterprises if one is to be increasingly successful from year to year.

Occasionally a quantity of fruit which will not meet the rigid requirements of the canning business can be turned into preserves, jellies or fruit juices. Preserves and jellies should be marketed in glass, and fruit juices in bottles, although some manufacturers are now marketing some of these products in fiber cups. This line of products will require some additional equipment, but there is a steady demand for such homemade things and many women are deriving profits through the sale of their tastily prepared jellies, just as pickles and condiments have lined the pocketbooks of ambitious housewives before now.

Home canning for the market is essentially a matter of specializing and of giving the consumer a better product than he is accustomed to purchase. Too much emphasis cannot be placed upon the maintenance of a high standard for home-canned goods. Care should be taken that every jar measures up to a rigid standard, for a single one which falls below grade will neutralize the reputation and standing obtained by the sale of a dozen jars of perfect product. A quality is necessary which will warrant a money-back guarantee on every jar.

THE USE OF LABELS IN CANNING

Labels for both tin cans and glass jars should tell the truth as to the quality, weight and kind of product within the pack. Before adopting a trade-mark and label, consult the Bureau of Chemistry, U.S. Department of Agriculture, Washington, D.C., as to label requirements for canned goods prepared for the market.

It pays to show samples of all your canned goods at county and state fairs. You may win many premiums. Goods which are canned with preservatives should be debarred from all exhibits.

PACKING GLASS FOR SHIPPING

Wrap each glass or jar separately in rumpled newspapers or excelsior and pack in barrels or boxes. Line these containers with papers or excelsior.

Strong corrugated parcel post boxes can be obtained for this purpose. Wrap each jar with excelsior or paper before putting it in its proper section. If sending large amounts send all boxes or all barrels, do not mix them,—sending half barrels and half boxes—as large concerns like uniform packages.

PACKING TIN FOR SHIPPING

Two dozen cans is the regulation shipping case. Have the shipping boxes of uniform size. Put the two dozen cans in the box and nail on the top. Be exceedingly careful not to drive nails into the cans. On both ends of the box paste labels such as are on the cans, telling what the contents of the box are.

Address the box carefully using marking ink or a regulation tag. If a tag, tack with small tacks on the top of the box. Write your own name and address on the tag *distinctly* as the sender. Be as careful of the tacks as you were of the nails. Always get a receipt from your express agent if shipping by express as this will be necessary in case of non-receipt of goods.

Send to the concern or individual to whom you are sending the goods a list of the things you have sent. This is called an invoice. Keep a copy of the invoice for yourself so if any question arises you will know what you are talking about.

SHIPPING TERMS

C.O.D. means collect on delivery. The purchaser pays the price of the products to the transportation company before they are delivered.

F.O.B. means free on board. For instance: if you send a shipment of canned goods to Chicago at $6.00 per case f.o.b. Charles City it means that you deliver the canned goods to the freight depot at Charles City and the purchaser pays both the price per case and the freight. If you deliver them f.o.b. Chicago it means you deliver them to the freight depot at Charles City and also pay the freight to Chicago.

Bill of Lading with Sight Draft Attached is a call for the money before the purchaser can take the products from the freight office.

Drop Shipment. If a wholesale firm requests that you ship direct to another firm buying from him, thus avoiding two shipments, this is called a drop shipment.

Lot Shipment. If you ship two or more barrels or cases as a "lot shipment" to the same destination they may be sent at a cheaper rate than if each were shipped separately.

LIST OF FIRMS FURNISHING SUPPLIES FOR CANNING, DRYING, PRESERVING, ETC

HOME AND CLUB COÖPERATIVE CANNING OUTFITS AND DEVICES Butler Manufacturing Co. Kansas City, Mo., and Minneapolis, Minn. Hot water and steam
and pressure canners. Carolina Metal Products Co. Wilmington, N.C.　"　"　" H.P. Chandlee Sons Co., Baltimore, Md. Hot water canners. Farm Canning Machine Co. Meridian, Miss.　"　"　" Favorite Manufacturing Co. Tamps, Florida Water-seal canners. Florida Metal Products Jacksonville, Fla. Water-seal canners. Griffith & Turner Co. 205-207 N. Pace St., Baltimore, Md. Steam canners. Halftime Cooker Co. 7556 Oglesby Avenue, Chicago, Ill. Pressure canners. Hall Canner Co. Grand Rapids, Mich. Hot water bath canners. Henninger & Ayes Mfg. Co 80-82 N. 5th Street, Portland, Ore. Steam pressure canners. Home Canner Manufacturing Co. Hickory, N.C. Hot water canners. E.F. Kirwan & Co. Baltimore, Md.
　"　"　" Modern Canner Co. Chattanooga, Tenn.
　"　"　" Monarch Manufacturing Co. Chattanooga, Tenn.　"　"　" Northwestern Steel & Iron Wks. Eau Claire, Wis. canners. Steam pressure Phillips & Buttorff Mfg. Co. Nashville, Tenn. Hot water canners. Pressure Cooker Co. Denver, Colo. Aluminum steam pressure
cookers and canners. T.H. Raney Chapel Hill, N.C. Hot water canners. A.K. Robins & Co. Baltimore, Md. Steam pressure canners Royal Supply Co. Cincinnati, Ohio Steam process canners. Southern Canner and Evaporator Co. Chattanooga, Tenn. Hot

water canners Sprague Canning Machinery Co. 222
No. Wabash Ave., Chicago, Ill. Steam pressure
canners. F.S. Stahl 212 N. 4th Street, Quincy, Ill.
Hot water canners. Standard Water-Seal Canner Co.
17 N. 2nd Street, Philadelphia, Pa. Water-seal
canners. Utility Company Hickory, N.C. Hot water
canners. Willson Canner Company Louisville, Ky.,
and No. 8 G St., N.W. Washington, D.C. Water-
seal and
and pressure canners.

HOME EVAPORATORS, DRYERS, AND
EQUIPMENT FOR DRYING American Paring
Machine Co 1231 Callowhill St., Philadelphia, Pa.
Peeler Harry Bentz Engineering Co. 90 West St.,
New York City Dryer G.S. Blakekslee & Company,
2806 Quinn St., Chicago, Ill. " H.P. Chandlee Sons
Co., Baltimore, Md. " Enterprise Mfg. Co., 3rd and
Dauphin Sts., Philadelphia, Pa. Slicer Edw. B.
Fahrney, Waynesboro, Pa. " Gordon Engineering
Corporaton 39 Cortlandt St., New York City " The
Grange Sales Association, Lafayette Bldg.,
Philadelphia, Pa. " Hunter Dry Kiln Co.
Indianapolis, Ind. Dryer Imperial Machine
Company, 108 West 34th St., N.Y. City Cuber Lake
Breeze Motor Co., 564 W. Monroe St., Chicago
Dryer Philadelphia Drying Machinery Co. Stekley
St., above Westmoreland, Philadelphia, Pa. "
Philadelphia Textile Machinery Co. Sixth St. and
Tabor Road, Philadelphia, Pa. " Phillips & Buttorff
Mfg. Co., Nashville, Tenn. " John E. Smith's Sons
Co., Buffalo, N.Y. Cuber Southern Evaporator Co.,
Chattanooga, Tenn. " F.S. Stahl, 212 N. 4th St.,
Quincy, Ill. " N.R. Streeter Company, Rochester,

N.Y. Dryer N.R. Streeter & Co., Rochester, N.Y. "
B.F. Sturtevant Company, Hyde Park Dist., Boston,
Mass. Peeler Stutzman Mfg. Company, Ligonier,
Ind. " H.G.W. Young Co., 61 Hanover St., Boston,
Mass. Cuber

MECHANICAL SEALS AND SEALERS FOR
TIN AND GLASS American Metal Cap Co.,
Summit St. and Commercial Wharf, Brooklyn, N.Y.
Metal bottle caps. American Pure Food Process Co.,
Greenmount Avenue and Preston St., Baltimore,
Md. Mechanical sealer for glass jars. Bowers Can
Seal Company, 146 Summer St., Boston, Mass.
Automatic can sealers for tin cans. Burpe Can
Sealer Co., 215 W. Huron St., Chicago. Tin can
sealer and opener. Columbia Specialty Co.,
Baltimore, Md. Metal bottle caps. Crown Cork and
Seal Co., Baltimore, Chicago, San Francisco, and
other cities Sanitary metal bottle caps and sealers.
The Enterprise Mfg. Co., Philadelphia, Pa. Bottle
cappers from 3 in. to 14 in. Frazer & Co., 50
Church Street, New York City Mechanical hand
sealer for sanitary cans. Henninger & Ayes Mfg.
Co., 47 1st Street, Portland, Ore. Automatic can
sealers for tin cans. States Metals Co., 30 Church
Street, New York City Hand sealers for sanitary
cans.

STEAMERS Aluminum Cooking Utensil Co. New
Kensington, Pa. Toledo Cooker Co. Toledo, Ohio.
Wilmot, Castle & Co. Rochester, N.Y.

HEATING DEVICES, LIFTING CRATES, AND
OTHER LABOR-SAVING DEVICES L.B. Allen
Co. Chicago, Ill. 4517 No. Lincoln St., Commercial
flux. Biddle-Gaumer Co. Philadelphia, Pa. Patent
canners. H.P. Chandlee Sons Co. Baltimore, Md.
" " " Fagley & Halpen Philadelphia, Pa.
" " " Handy Mfg. Co. Maritime Bldg., Seattle
Wash., and
No. 208 Wabash Ave., Chicago, Ill. Individual jar
holders. Kerr Glass Mfg. Co. Sand Springs, Okla.
Duplex fork. Manning, Bowman & Co. Meriden,
Conn. Alcholite stoves. Parker Wire Goods Co.
Worcester, Mass. Lifting tray for jars. Pearce Co.
Albion, Mich. Racks and lifters. W.H. Schaefer Co.
Toledo, Ohio. Fruit jar wrench.

LABELS, STICKERS, SHIELDS AND BADGES
Camden Curtain and Embroidery Co. Camden, New
Jersey. R.P. Clarke & Co. Washington, D.C.
Dennison Mfg. Co. Boston, Mass. U.S. Printing and
Lithograph Co. Cincinnati, Ohio.

TIN CANS AND GLASS JARS American Can Co.
New York City. Tin cans. Ball Bros. Glass Mfg. Co.
Muncie, Ind. Screw top and glass-top jars Ben
Schloss San Francisco, Cal. Glass jars. Buck Glass
Co. Baltimore, Md. Glass jars. Chesapeake Glass
Co. Baltimore, Md. Glass jars. Continental Can Co.
Chicago, Ill. Tin cans. Frazer & Co. 50 Church St.,
N.Y.C. Sanitary cans. Hazel-Atlas Glass Co.
Wheeling, W. Va. Glass-top jars. Johnson-Morse
Can Co. Wheeling, W. Va. Tin cans. Kearns-
Gorsuch Bottle Co. Zanesville, Ohio. Glass jars.

Kerr Glass Mfg. Co. Sand Springs, Okla. Suction
seal and Mason jars. E.F. Kirwan Co. Baltimore,
Md. Tin cans. A.K. Robins & Co. Baltimore, Md.
Tin cans and general equipment. Schramm Glass
Mfg. Co. St. Louis, Mo. Suction seal and screw top
jars. Smalley Fruit Jar Co. 26 Dock Sq., Boston,
Mass. Glass-top jars. Southern Can Co. Baltimore,
Md. Tin cans. F.S. Stahl Quincy, Ill.   "   "   "
Staunton Jar Corporation*N.Y.* Ellicott Sq, Buffalo,
Vacuum seal jars. United States Can Co. Cincinnati,
Ohio Tin cans. Virginia Can Co. Buchanan, Va.
  "   "   " Wheeling Can Co. Wheeling, W.Va.
  "   "   "

RUBBER RINGS FOR COLD-PACK CANNING
Acme Rubber Co. Trenton, N.J. Boston Woven
Hose & Rubber Co. Boston, Mass. United States
Rubber Co. Cleveland, Ohio.

GLASS BOTTLES AND OTHER CONTAINERS
FOR FRUIT JUICES, CATSUP, ETC. Adams
Brothers Co. Chicago, Ill. Atlantic Bottle Co. 90
West Broadway, N.Y. City. Berney-Bond Glass Co.
Bradford, Pa. Cape May Glass Co. Cape May Court
House, N.J. Cumberland Glass Mfg. Co. Bridgeton,
N.J. The Federal Glass Co. Columbus, Ohio C.L.
Flaccus Glass Co. Pittsburgh, Pa. Glenshaw Glass
Co. Glenshaw, Pa. C.C. Goss Glass Co., Mfg. Agts.
172 Fulton St., New York City. Hocking Glass Co.
Lancaster, Ohio. Imperial Glass Co. Charleroi, Pa.
Indiana Glass Co. Dunkirk, Ind. D.C. Jenkins Glass
Co. Kokomo, Ind. Kearns-Gorsuch Bottle Co.
Zanesville, Ohio. North Wheeling Glass Bottle Co.

Wheeling, W.Va. Ripley & Co. Connellsville, Pa.
Schramm Glass Mfg. Co. St. Louis, Mo. Sheffield
Glass Bottle Co. Sheffield, Pa. The Sterling Glass
Co. Lapel, Ind. Turner Brothers Co. Terre Haute,
Ind. United States Glass Co. Salem, N.J. Upland
Flint Bottle Co. Upland, Ind. Western Bottle Mfg.
Co. West end Randolph St. Bridge, Chicago, Ill.
Whitall-Tatum Co. 410-416 Race St., Philadelphia,
Pa. Wightman Bottle & Glass Mfg. Co. Parkers
Landing, Pa. Williamstown Glass Co.
Williamstown, N.J. Woodbury Glass Co.
Winchester, Ind.

GLASS BOTTLES SEALED WITH CORKS AND
METAL CAPS Acme Glass Co. Olean, N.Y.
Binghamton Glass Co. Binghamton, N.Y. C.L.
Flaccus Glass Co. Pittsburgh, Pa. Hazel-Atlas Glass
Co. Wheeling, W.Va. Imperial Glass Co. Charleroi,
Pa. Jeanette Glass Co. Jeanette, Pa. Kearns-Gorsuch
Bottle Co. Zanesville, Ohio. North Baltimore Bottle
Glass Co. Terre Haute, Ind. Turner Brothers Co.
Terre Haute, Ind. Whitney Glass Works Glassboro,
N.J.

EARTHENWARE AND STONEWARE
CONTAINERS Buckel Pottery Co. White Hall, Ill.
Buckeye Pottery Co. Macomb, Ill. Burley and
Winter Pottery Co. Crooksville, Ohio. Hawthorn
Pottery Co. Hawthorn, Pa. Logan Pottery Co.
Logan, Ohio Louisville Pottery Co. Louisville, Ky.
Muskingum Pottery Co. White Cottage, Ohio.
Nashville Pottery Co. Nashville, Tenn. Nelson
McCly Sanitary Hardware Co. Roseville, Ohio.

Paducah Pottery Co. Paducah, Ky. Pfaltzaraff
Pottery Co. York, Pa. Ransbottom Bros., Pottery
Co. Roseville, Ohio. Red Wing Union Stoneware
Co. Red Wing, Minn. Star Stoneware Co.
Crooksville, Ohio. Uhl Pottery Co. Evansville, Ind.
Western Stoneware Co. Monmouth, Ill. White Hall
Sewer Pipe & Stoneware Co. White Hall, Ill.

FIBRE AND PAPER CANS AND BOTTLES

American Can Co. 447 W. 14th, New York City,
and Chicago, Ill. The American Paper Can Co.
Washington, D.C. The Canister Company of New
Jersey Phillipsburg, N.J. Continental Paper Bag Co.
17 Battery Place, New York City. Cordley & Hayes
7-9 Leonard St., New York City. The Empire Paper
Tube and Box Co. 155 Bank St., New York City.
The Hygeia Paper Container Co. 2106 Auburn
Ave., Toledo, Ohio. Moisture Proof Fibre Can Co.
Detroit, Mich. Mono-Service Co. Newark, N.J.
Samuel W. Moore & Sons 95 Liberty St., New
York City. National Paper Can Co. 576 Clinton St.,
Milwaukee, Wis. National Paper Products Co. San
Francisco, Cal. Pure Food Package Co. 200
Devonshire St., Boston, Mass. The Purity Paper
Bottle Co., Inc. 1341 S. Capitol St., Washington,
D.C. W.C. Ritchie & Co. 400 S. Green St.,
Chicago, Ill. Sanitary Paper Bottle Co. Sandusky,
Ohio. Single Service Package Corp. of America 326
Hudson St., New York City. St. Louis Paper Can &
Tube Co. 4400 Union Boulevard, St. Louis, Mo.
The Standard Package Co. 50 State St., Boston,
Mass. Washington Paper Can Co. 425 12th St.,
N.W., Washington, D.C. Weis Fibre Container
Corporation Monroe, Mich.

FOIL-LINED PAPER BAGS Thomas M. Royal &
Co. Bryn Mawr, Pa.

DELIVERY CONTAINERS FOR EGGS,
VEGETABLES, DRIED FOOD PRODUCTS,
ETC. Bloomer Bros. Co. Newark, New York.
Doane Carton Co. 920 N. Market St., St. Louis, Mo.
Hinde & Dauch Paper Co. Sandusky, Ohio. Mono-
Service Co. Newark, N.J. National Paper Products
Co. San Francisco, Cal. Thomas M. Royal & Co.
Bryn Mawr, Pa. W.A. Schurmann & Co. 365 E. Ill.
St., Chicago, Ill. Sefton Mfg. Co. 1301 W. 35th St.,
Chicago, Ill. Thompson & Norris Co. Brooklyn,
N.Y. United States Corrugated Fibre Box Co.
Roosevelt Ave., Indianapolis, Ind. Weis Fibre
Container Corporation Monroe, Mich.

PARCEL POST EGG CONTAINERS O.B.
Andrews Co. Chattanooga, Tenn. H.K. Brunner 45
Harrison St., New York City. J.C. Bulis Mfg. Co.
1122-28 S. 12th St., St Louis, Mo. Continental
Paper Bag Co. 17 Battery Place, New York City.
Cummer Mfg. Co. Cadillac, Mich. Day Collapsible
Box Co., Inc. Washington Grove, Md. Empire
Printing & Box Co. Atlanta, Ga. F.B. Foster & Co.
2447 Locust St., Philadelphia, Pa. Robert Gair Co.
Brooklyn, N.Y. Hinde & Dauch Paper Co.
Sandusky, Ohio. Ohio No-Break Carrier Co. 702
Mercantile Library Bldg., Cincinnati, Ohio. Sefton
Mfg. Corporation 1301 W. 35th St., Chicago, Ill.
Self-Locking Carton Co. 437 E. Illinois St.,

Chicago, Ill. Thompson & Norris Co. Concord &
Prince Sts., Brooklyn,N.Y.
 Boston, Mass., and Brookville, Ind. U.S. Safety
Egg Carrier Co. Newark, N.Y. Wallace Egg Carrier
Co. 451 3rd St., San Francisco, Cal.

 MISCELLANEOUS CORRUGATED BOARD
CONTAINERS American Can Co. New York City
and Chicago, Ill. J.C. Bulis Mfg. Co. 1122-28 S.
12th St., St. Louis, Mo. Empire Printing & Box Co.
Atlanta, Ga. Federal Glass Co. Columbus, Ohio
Robert Gair Co. Brooklyn, N.Y. Hinde & Dauch
Paper Co. Sandusky, Ohio National Paper Products
Co. San Francisco, Cal. Sefton Mfg. Corporation
1301 W. 35th St., Chicago, Ill. Thompson & Norris
Co. Concord and Prince Sts., Brooklyn,N.Y.
 Boston, Mass., and Brookville, Ind. U.S.
Corrugated Fibre Box Co. 1315 Martindale Ave.,
Indianapolis, Ind.

 THERMOMETERS FOR OVEN, CANDY AND
SUGAR Taylor Instrument Companies Rochester,
N.Y.

Made in the USA
San Bernardino, CA
11 December 2015